Running a Charity

Third Edition

Running a Charity

Third Edition

Alison MacLennan
Radcliffe Chambers
11 New Square
London

JORDANS

Published by
Jordan Publishing Limited
21 St Thomas Street
Bristol BS1 6JS

British Library Cataloguing-in-Publication Data

A catalogue record for this book is available from the British Library.

ISBN 978 1 84661 093 6

Typeset by Letterpart Ltd, Reigate, Surrey

Printed in Great Britain by Antony Rowe Limited, Chippenham, Wiltshire

PREFACE TO THE THIRD EDITION

Since the last edition of this book was published in 1997 the Charities Act 2006 has received Royal Assent. The first provisions of the new act came into force in February 2007 with the remaining provisions due to come into force over the next few years. The new legislation extensively changes the existing law. In particular there are new rules on charitable purposes and the Charity Commission will be subject to reform.

The model documents in Appendix A have been drafted and updated by Francesca Quint for the Charity Law Association, and have been approved by the Charity Commission. They are reproduced with the Association's permission.

Alison MacLennan

February 2008

CONTENTS

Preface to the Third Edition   v

Chapter 1
Introduction   1
What is a charity?   1
   England and Wales   1
   Scotland   2
   Exclusively charitable purposes   2
Who is a charity trustee?   3
Responsibilities of charity trustees   4
   Public trust   4
   Conflict   4
   Delegation   5
   Contracts with third parties   5
   Other duties   6
Charitable status – examples   6

Chapter 2
Constitutional Requirements   9
Setting up   9
Choosing the legal form   10
Registration in England and Wales   11
   Exempt charities   11
   Excepted charities   12
   Registration pack   12
   Name of charity   12
   HM Revenue and Customs   13
   Registration number   13
   Significance of registration   13
Registration in Scotland   14
Changing the constitution   14
   Alteration to memorandum and articles of association   14
   Express power of alteration   15
   Alternative procedures   15
      Statutory power   15
      Scheme   16
   Reviewing aims and procedures   17
   The new governing instrument   17

Amalgamation   18
    Transfer of assets   18
        Statutory power   18
        Scheme   19
Winding up   19
    Express power to wind up   20
    Statutory power   20
    Scheme   21
    Powers of Commission or Court of Session to wind up   21
Cy-près schemes – examples   21

Chapter 3
Money and Property   **23**
Accounting   23
Accounts and record-keeping   23
    Structure   23
    Small charities   24
    Formats   25
    Policies   25
    The annual report   25
    Branches   26
Independent audit   27
Tax and rates   28
    Income and capital gains   28
    Property used for charitable purposes   28
    Payments from supporters   28
    Payroll Deduction Scheme   29
    Gifts   29
    HM Revenue and Customs guidance   29
Insurance   29
    Fire, other damage and theft   29
    Vandalism and terrorism   30
    Public and employer's liability   30
    Fidelity insurance   30
    Particular risks   30
    Liability insurance   30
    Other means of financial protection   31
Investment   31
    Common investment funds   31
    Powers of investment   32
        Statutory powers (unincorporated charities)   32
        Schemes   32
    Advice on investments   33
        Investment advisers   33
    Holding of investments   33
        Incorporation   34
    Land investment   34

Land and buildings   34
  Holding of land   35
    Certificate of incorporation (England and Wales)   35
    Land vested in the Official Custodian (England and Wales)   36
  Sale, exchange or leasing of land (England and Wales)   36
    New procedure   37
    Formalities   37
  Mortgage of land   38
  Disposal of land (Scotland)   38
Making grants   38
  Objective of grant   38
  Applications for assistance   39
  Policy guidelines   39
Raising funds   40
  Managing fundraising   41
  Methods of fundraising   41
  Restrictions on fundraising   41
  Fundraising records   42
  Fundraising agreements   43
    England and Wales   43
    Scotland   44
  Offences   44
Accepting gifts and legacies   44
  Refusal to accept gifts   45
  Gifts subject to conditions   45
    Failure of purpose   46
    'General charitable intention'   46
    Identifiable donors   46
  Avoiding failure   47
Patrons and sponsors   47
  'Commercial participators'   48
Trading   48
  Trading activities as adjunnct to charitable purpose   48
  Trading for the purpose of raising funds   48

Chapter 4
Management   **51**
Choosing trustees   51
Trustee meetings   52
  Preparation   53
  Quorum   53
  Chairmanship   53
  Minutes   54
  Frequency of trustee meetings   54
Dealing with professionals   55
  Choosing a professional   55
    Fees   55
    Relationship between adviser and trustees   55

Effectiveness   56
Problems with advisers   56
Mistakes to avoid   57
Particular specialists   57
Beauty parades   58
Employees and volunteers   59
Interviewing candidates   59
Freedom from insecurity   59
Freedom from annoyance   60
Encouragement or praise when deserved   60
Support for weaknesses   60
Training   60
Fairness   60
Remuneration (including pension rights)   60
Health and safety legislation   61
Relationship between director and trustees   61
Good management   61
Time   62
Contract culture   62
Coherence   62
Charity consultants   63
Stationery and equipment   63
Cost   64
Computers   64
Premises   65
Appearance of premises   65
Regulations   65
Listed buildings   66
Moving premises   66
Neighbours   66
Training   67
Self-help   67
Academic institutions   67
Technical skills training   68
Special courses   68
Opportunities for staff   68
Informal training   68
Troubleshooting   69
Physical emergencies   70
Insurance   70
Negligence   70
Tenants' defaults   70
Compensation   70
Problems   70
Running out of money   70
Charity Commission inquiry (England and Wales)   71
Lord Advocate's powers (Scotland)   72
Mediation   72

Chapter 5
Europe **75**
How charities fit in 75
   Social economy 75
European law 76
   Treaties 76
   Regulations 76
   Directives 76
   Decisions 77
   Recommendations and Opinions 77
European institutions 77
   Council of Ministers 77
   Committees of Permanent Representatives 77
   European Council 78
   Commission 78
   Directorates General 78
   European Parliament 78
   Committees 79
   Economic and Social Committee 79
   Committee of the Regions 80
   European Foundation 80
   Council of Europe 80
Interaction 80
   Commission 80
   European Parliament 81
   European Social Committee 82
   European Foundation 82
   Non-governmental organisations 82
   European programmes 82
Networks and umbrella bodies 83
Recent developments in EU law relating to charities 84
   EC Consultation 84
   Cross-border charitable giving 84

Appendix A
Model Documents **85**

Appendix B
Trustees Annual Reporting **141**

Appendix C
Official Addresses **149**

Appendix D
Helpful Organisations **153**

Appendix E
Further Reading 157

Index 161

CHAPTER 1

INTRODUCTION

1.1 WHAT IS A CHARITY?

The word 'charity' has a general meaning in ordinary speech and a special meaning in law. This book is concerned with charity in that special, legal sense.

1.1.1 England and Wales

Since the time of Queen Elizabeth I and before, certain purposes have been regarded by English law as worthy of favourable treatment: the courts and the Charity Commission will help to enforce them and prevent abuses through trust law. In addition, the rules which normally require a trust to be brought to an end after a certain length of time ('the perpetuity period') and which restrict the number of trustees, do not apply to charities and, because the purposes themselves must be beneficial to the public, organisations devoted to them are given favourable tax and rating treatment. The courts and the Commission also have the power, by means of a tool called a 'scheme', to alter a charity's purposes to bring them up to date or to make them workable.

A list of charitable purposes appears in the Charities Act 2006, s 2(2), and every charity must be formed for the benefit of the public. It is for the Commission to test whether or not an organisation is beneficial to the public. If a charitable purpose is for the benefit of the public it may be charitable if it falls within any of the following descriptions of purposes:

'(a) the prevention or relief of poverty;
(b) the advancement of education;
(c) the advancement of religion;
(d) the advancement of health or the saving of lives;
(e) the advancement of citizenship or community development;
(f) the advancement of the arts, culture, heritage or science;
(g) the advancement of amateur sport;
(h) the advancement of human rights, conflict resolution or reconciliation or the promotion of religious or racial harmony or equality and diversity;
(i) the advancement of environmental protection or improvement;

(j) the relief of those in need by reason of youth, age, ill-health, disability, financial hardship or other disadvantage;

(k) the advancement of animal welfare;

(l) the promotion of the efficiency of the armed forces of the Crown, or of the efficiency of the police, fire and rescue services or ambulance services;

(m) any other purposes within subsection (4) [ie purposes already recognised as charitable or by virtue of the Recreational Charities Act 1958].'

Every charitable purpose will come within one (or more) of these categories, but not every purpose which is within these categories is necessarily charitable. Deciding whether a given purpose is charitable depends on legal precedent and analogy from legal precedent. Sometimes, a purpose which was not regarded as charitable in the past will be accepted as charitable as times change. An example of this is the promotion of racial harmony, which was accepted as a charitable purpose only during the 1980s. The opposite can also occur. Even if an organisation is charitable at its inception each charity must ensure that it remains beneficial to the public each year.

1.1.2 Scotland

In Scotland, which has a different legal system whose origins can be traced back to Roman law, the meaning of 'charity' has traditionally been less technical and, for most purposes, equivalent to the relief of poverty. However, since the Charities and Trustee Investment (Scotland) Act 2005 there has been a 'charity test'. To pass the test an organisation must have one or more of the purposes set out in the 2005 Act, provide public benefit in Scotland, not be a political party and its constitution must not allow its property to be distributed for non-charitable purposes. Further, the activities of the organisation should not be controlled or directed by government ministers and the charity's name must not be misleading, too similar to an existing charity's name, or offensive. Information and guidance connected with Scottish charities can be obtained from the new Office of the Scottish Charity Regulator ('OSCR').

Registered Scottish charities are treated in the same way by HM Revenue and Customs ('HMRC'). Policy issues relating to charity law and regulation are dealt with by the Scottish Executive.

1.1.3 Exclusively charitable purposes

A charity, a trust or organisation must be established for exclusively charitable purposes. It is not enough that some of its purposes are charitable if other purposes are commercial, political or for the benefit of private individuals, or even if they are simply good causes which do not come within the legal concept of charity.

As long as the purposes are exclusively charitable it does not matter what form the trust or organisation takes, or what assets it has, or how many people are involved in running it. Charities come in all shapes and sizes. Of course, there are tried and tested forms of trust and organisation and, depending on what the charity aims to achieve, the activities it is involved in and the resources available, there are optimum numbers for the governing body, staff and so on. There is also a new form of charity which has been created by the Charities Act 2006, known as a charitable incorporated organisation ('CIO').

These matters are discussed in more detail in Chapter 2.

1.2 WHO IS A CHARITY TRUSTEE?

The expression 'charity trustees' is defined in the Charities Act 1993 as meaning the body of people responsible for the management and control of the administration of a charity. It can also be termed the charity's 'governing body'. In the Charities Accounts (Scotland) Regulations 1992, SI 1992/2165, the word 'trustees' is defined in relation to any recognised body as the persons 'in management or control' of that body. The function of this body, rather than the name given to it, determines whether they are the trustees, or charity trustees. In this book, the expression 'charity trustees' or 'trustees' will be used as a shorthand expression for all those who constitute a charity's governing body, whether they are described as trustees, governors, feoffees, committee members, council members, directors, board members or some other designation. It does not include employees of the governing body, although much of what is said about trustees is directly relevant to the responsibilities of senior staff and officers of a charity.

Some charities have more than one tier of responsibility within their governing structure. For example, the function of holding the legal title to property is often allocated to a body or group of people separate from the decision-makers themselves and (confusingly) the property-holders may be called 'trustees' in the charity's constitution. It is also not uncommon for day-to-day management decisions to be delegated to a small number of the governing body, often called the 'executive committee'.

Anyone who becomes involved in a formal capacity in the running of a charity should be quite clear from the outset whether or not he or she has the responsibilities of a charity trustee. In cases of doubt, the Charity Commission (in England and Wales) or a professional legal adviser will be able to clarify the position. All charity trustees must act reasonably and, under the Trustee Act 2000, there is a new duty to act prudently when investing charity funds.

1.3 RESPONSIBILITIES OF CHARITY TRUSTEES

A trustee shares responsibility with his or her co-trustees. Unless there is a specific provision in the governing instrument requiring a different proportion, decisions are taken on a simple majority vote of those present at a meeting, usually with a casting vote for the chairman of the meeting. All the trustees are bound by a decision properly taken. Attendance at trustees' meetings is, therefore, one of the main duties, and someone whose other commitments do not permit regular attendance should not be a trustee. Many charities must have a minimum number of trustees attending meetings in order to act.

1.3.1 Public trust

Trusteeship of a charity is a public trust, which calls for a high degree of integrity. Trusteeship cannot validly be undertaken by a person who is under 18 years of age or who is suffering from mental incapacity. There is no place on a charity's trustee body for someone who has an ulterior motive, whether this is political or commercial or a private benefit for the trustee or someone connected with the trustee. It is essential that the trustees are able to satisfy an enquirer that all decisions are taken in good faith in the interests of the charity itself. People who have been convicted of offences involving deception or dishonesty (unless the convictions are spent), or who have been disqualified from acting as company directors or removed involuntarily from previous charity trusteeships, or have been made bankrupt or entered into a voluntary arrangement with creditors, are generally unsuitable to be trustees. Under English law, they cannot lawfully become charity trustees and may suffer criminal penalties if they do. A professional legal adviser or (in England and Wales) the Charity Commission will clarify the situation in case of doubt if given the full facts. In suitable cases, the Commission will waive this restriction. Recent changes allow someone who was disqualified from being a charity trustee over five years ago to apply to the Commission for approval to become a trustee again.

1.3.2 Conflict

A trustee who stands to gain, however innocently, from a decision of the charity's governing body, or who finds that there is any conflict between his or her duty to the charity and his or her personal interests, should disclose this and take no part in the decision. If the conflict is sufficiently serious or is likely to be prolonged, the trustee concerned may have to avoid attending meetings for a time, or even resign his or her trusteeship. If, however, the trustees as a whole are convinced that the resignation would not be in the charity's interests, they may seek a special dispensation from the Charity Commission (or, in Scotland, the OSCR). If a trustee is found to have benefited from his or her position as a trustee, the Commission may make an order requiring the trustee to restore to the charity any private gains enjoyed. If a trustee appears to be able to offer services to the charity, the charity may enter into a contract for the trustee to provide those services provided every effort is made to tender the work to others also, and to manage any conflict of interest by ensuring that that particular trustee is not involved in the decision to award the contract.

Conflicts can also arise between a trustee's duty to the charity and some other public obligation. This is not uncommon because those who are willing to shoulder responsibilities usually tend to have further responsibilities placed upon them. Charity trustees are often local councillors, school governors or trustees of other charities. Alternatively, trustees may be appointed by outside bodies which have an interest of their own in the area in which the charity's work lies. If the trustee is appointed by, or a member of, another body, he or she must remember that, as a trustee, his or her duty to the charity overrides all other obligations. If an irreconcilable conflict arises, he or she may have to avoid taking part in decisions of the charity, or attending meetings or, in extreme cases, to resign from one or other position.

1.3.3 Delegation

Trustees must not delegate their responsibilities, except insofar as is permitted by the governing instrument of the charity and by the general law. Thus, trustees take personal responsibility for all major decisions made in their name and, if they allow someone else to decide something on their behalf, they are legally responsible for that decision. They must know, therefore, what is going on within the charity at all times, and have workable procedures for dealing with emergencies.

Many charities employ staff to carry out the day-to-day management of the charity and employ specialist managers to take care of property or investments. It is vitally important that staff and managers should have clear policy guidelines to work to and ready access to the trustees should the need arise. Good practice is for the trustees to decide in advance what their policies should be and to decide on written policy documents.

1.3.4 Contracts with third parties

Contracts made with third parties on the charity's behalf are the legal responsibility of the contracting parties. Where the charity or the trustee body is an incorporated body, such as a limited liability company, the body itself, as a legal person in its own right, is the contracting party and individual members of the body will not, generally, be personally liable. (There is an exception where a company is operating whilst technically insolvent.) Where, however, the charity and the trustees are unincorporated, the trustees themselves will be the contracting parties and if the charity is not able to meet its commitment, the trustees will normally be personally liable. Contracting as a trustee does not, itself, limit a trustee's potential liability. This underlines the need for trustees to take care never to enter into any commitment on the charity's behalf which the charity's resources will not meet, unless the trustees are prepared to underwrite it personally.

Other situations and activities, such as ownership of property, operations on land or buildings, the employment of staff or fundraising events can also give rise to legal liabilities or other costs. It is wise, in order to protect both the charity and the individual trustees, to insure fully against all usual risks.

1.3.5   Other duties

The law imposes a number of more specific duties on charity trustees, for example the requirement to keep accounts and to produce an annual report, to supply certain information and documents to the Charity Commission (or, in Scotland, the OSCR), and (in the case of English charities) to seek the Commission's consent to certain transactions. These specific duties are dealt with in detail later in this book.

Finally, it is worth while for every trustee to bear in mind that the charity has a reputation of its own, which is dependent on the trustees and their staff. A charity may be a landlord, an employer, a neighbour or a provider of services. The law does not permit a charity to operate otherwise than in furtherance of its purposes, but there is nothing to prevent it from acting efficiently, fairly and reasonably in its relations with the rest of the world while doing so.

1.4   CHARITABLE STATUS – EXAMPLES

These are some contrasting examples of decisions by the English courts and the Charity Commission on charitable status which illustrate the fine distinctions which sometimes have to be drawn in interpreting the law. Many textbooks have discussions about what has or has not been accepted as charitable. Perhaps the most useful tool for gaining a flavour of what is charitable is the Register of Charities itself. This is maintained by the Commission and is available online. The website has an efficient search engine which allows the Register to be searched by reference to key words or areas.

Since the passing of the Charities Act 2006 there have been few controversial decisions. The examples given below are decisions made before the 2006 Act was passed:

(1)   A gift for paying for holidays for low-paid employees of a particular firm was held to be charitable, even though the beneficiaries were not a section of the public (1914).

(2) A fund set up by a merchant bank to assist sick or convalescent employees was rejected by the Commission since the beneficiaries were not a section of the public and were not in financial need (circa 1980).

(3) A trust for the poor relatives of the founder was upheld as charitable (1995). This type of case is now regarded as exceptional and it is unlikely that new charities of this type will be entered on the Register of Charities.

(4) A trust under the will of Mrs Bernard Shaw for teaching the Irish the arts of conversation and self-control was held to be charitable as it was educational (1952).

(5) A trust under the will of Mr Bernard Shaw to construct a phonetic alphabet was held to be non-charitable because, although this would have increased knowledge, the will did not provide for the results to be communicated to the public and, in any case, the trust was considered to be political (1957).

(6) A gift by will to a Carmelite (ie enclosed) order of nuns was held to be non-charitable because, although this promoted a religious purpose, there could be no proven benefit to the public from private prayer (1949). (In Irish law the gift would be charitable).

(7) A gift to a synagogue which was open only to members was held to be charitable because the worshippers would go out into the community during the rest of the week and, thereby, spread the benefits of religious activities to the public (1966).

(8) A trust under the will of Mr Strakosch to improve relations between English and Dutch-speaking South Africans was held to be non-charitable because it was considered to be political (1952).

(9) A body established in Birmingham for the promotion of racial harmony within the local community was accepted as charitable by the Commission (1982).

(10) A rifle club and a pistol club were held not to be charities (1994).

(11) A Training Enterprise Council was held not to be a charity (1996).

CHAPTER 2

CONSTITUTIONAL REQUIREMENTS

2.1 SETTING UP

Forming a charity is comparable to the procreation of a child. First there is the general idea, then a decision and a series of meetings between the promoters, then a period of gestation and, finally, the day on which the new charity comes into formal existence. Usually, registration (or recognition) follows soon afterwards. Anything may go wrong at any stage until the formal establishment of the charity and, of course, in some instances the infant may be stillborn or, if not given proper care and nourishment, it may not survive to maturity.

Some of the excitement and emotional satisfaction associated with the birth of a child are also to be experienced in setting up a new charity. Equally, it has to be said, there are numerous pitfalls and the possibility that the promoters will disagree on the proper direction and development of the infant. In extreme cases there may be abandonment, negligence or an amicable parting of the ways. Unlike a parent, however, the promoter of a charity cannot be made financially liable for its future maintenance, although, if it does not survive he or she, if a trustee, may be required to see that it is duly interred.

The first task in establishing a charity is to determine its purposes, activities, the people who will be involved and the resources which will be available to it. This process, which may take some time, should enable a decision to be taken on the form which the charity will take. Where the charity is to be founded by an individual, a group of people or an existing organisation prepared to donate money at the outset, the classic form of *declaration of trust* will probably be the simplest and most convenient form of establishing the charity, since it allows considerable control to the founder (or founders). Where, however, a lot of fundraising activity is necessary and a larger number of people will be involved, it may not be practicable to proceed without building in a measure of 'democracy'. In that case, an *unincorporated charitable association* may be the most appropriate and flexible legal form. If the charity is to undertake activities involving the employment of a substantial number of staff, or if it will necessarily encounter commercial risks in carrying out its work, a *company limited by guarantee* may be the best solution. Examples of these older three forms of establishing a charity can be found in Appendix A. These are English precedents but may be adapted for use elsewhere.

Also included in Appendix A is a new form of incorporated charity called a *charitable incorporated organisation*. This type of charity enjoys its own corporate existence, like a company, but is regulated only by the Charity Commission and not by the Registrar of Companies. Regulations under the Charities Act 2006 prescribe the essential elements of the constitution of this type of organisation.

Some charities are established *by will* and it cannot be emphasised too strongly that, if this course is chosen, professional advice should be obtained before the will is made.

There are some other cases. Where the charity is to be a housing association, the best recognised legal form is an *industrial and provident society*. Where the charity is fortunate enough to have substantial patronage, a *Royal Charter* may be sought. Occasionally, a charity will be set up by an *Act of Parliament*.

A certain amount of help can be obtained from specialist organisations (some of which are listed in Appendices B and C), but it is generally advisable to seek independent professional advice before finalising the form of a new charity, and essential to do so if there is anything unusual in the proposals.

2.2   CHOOSING THE LEGAL FORM

It should be clear from the outset what the effect will be of choosing one form of establishing a charity over another. Once the charity has been set up the trustees and officers will be bound to observe its terms and follow the procedures which it lays down.

Under English law, the simplest form to set up and operate is the declaration of trust. The trust is not a separate person from its trustees and there are no special formalities apart from:

(1)   the necessity to have the original document stamped by the Stamp Office of HM Revenue and Customs ('HMRC'); and

(2)   the requirements of charity law, including registration in most cases.

Setting up a charitable trust in Scotland is now similar to the English and Welsh system. An organisation sends its trust document and an application form to the Office of the Scottish Charity Regulator ('OSCR') with the most recent available accounts and a description of the activities of the organisation. The OSCR will assess the application against the charity test and, if successful, the organisation will be entered on the Scottish Register of Charities.

An unincorporated charitable association can also be simple to operate in either jurisdiction, provided that the terms of the constitution are clear and workable. Again, no separate legal person is created and in this case there is no requirement for a stamp.

Running a charitable company limited by guarantee involves some operational technicalities and should not be undertaken lightly. First, the formalities on setting up the company necessitate registration as a company. It will, therefore, be desirable to use the services of a solicitor, accountant or company formation agent. The company is a separate legal person from those who run it. There are also a number of requirements under company law which will have to be observed in addition to the requirements of charity law. The company must have a registered office (an official address); it must have a company secretary; annual returns must be submitted to Companies House; accounts must be audited by a registered company auditor (however small the operations may be); a register of members must be kept and an annual general meeting of the members held. There is an important requirement *not* to continue to operate if the company is insolvent, ie if its assets are not sufficient to enable its debts and other liabilities to be met. Company law is underpinned by statutory offences.

A charitable incorporated organisation is a new form of charity whose structure is intended to relieve trustees of many of the complicated company law requirements.

2.3 REGISTRATION IN ENGLAND AND WALES

Most charities in England and Wales must be registered with the Charity Commission. The main exceptions are those classed as 'exempt charities', charities which do not have land or permanent capital or an income of at least £1,000 pa, places of worship registered under the Places of Worship Registration Act 1855 and 'excepted charities', such as voluntary schools.

2.3.1 Exempt charities

Exempt charities consist of certain major charities and types of charities listed in the Charities Act 1993, Sch 2. Apart from institutions such as the British Museum, English Heritage and the colleges of Eton and Winchester, they include universities, colleges, grant-maintained schools and charitable societies formed under the Industrial and Provident Societies Acts and charitable friendly societies. Exempt charities cannot register, are free from the supervision of the Charity Commission and are not subject to the new requirements on charity accounting. Instead, they are subject to other forms of supervision, such as the Higher Education Funding Council for England, which generally prescribe their own forms of accounting rules.

2.3.2   Excepted charities

Charities which do not need to register because they are 'excepted' from that requirement, for example voluntary schools, are subject to Charity Commission supervision and may be required to produce full accounts. The reason why they do not need to be registered is simply that there is a statutory record of their existence elsewhere.

2.3.3   Registration pack

If a charity will (or may) need to be registered it is sensible (and recognised as good practice) to consult the Charity Commission's registration pack before the draft governing instrument has been finalised. (It is, of course, not usually practicable to do this where the charity is established by will and its terms have already been settled and have come into legal effect by the time the trustees are aware of those terms.) The pack is available (free of charge) from the Commission and is designed to answer all the most usual queries a body of prospective trustees may have. It includes a questionnaire which is designed to assist the Commission in deciding whether or not to accept a charity for registration. The Commission ask the promoters of new charities (and the trustees of charities which have come into existence but have not been registered) to submit the completed questionnaire with two copies of the governing instrument, together with any other relevant materials, such as financial records. Considerable care should be exercised in completing the questionnaire, since the questions are not always fully understood on first reading and an inaccurate response can lead to misunderstanding and serious delay. In some cases, where an accepted model is not used, it is wise to send the Commission a *draft* of the proposed governing instrument and even seek an interview at their office to explain exactly what is proposed.

2.3.4   Name of charity

The Charity Commission will also consider the name of the new charity. If they find that it is the same as, or similar to, the name of an existing charity, they may require it to be changed. This applies to informal names and acronyms, as well as the formal, legal title of the charity. They may also require a new name to be chosen if the proposed name is misleading or offensive (see Appendix F).

2.3.5   HM Revenue and Customs

Unless the proposals are entirely straightforward and the governing instrument follows one of the recognised model forms, the Charity Commission will normally consult the Financial Intermediaries and Claims Office ('FICO') of HMRC before indicating whether they will accept the proposed charity for registration. This is because HMRC is a 'person interested' in the registration of a charity, in view of the tax consequences of charitable status. In many cases, the Commission's approval will be subject to specific alterations being made to the governing instrument. Very often, such suggested alterations are based on recognised forms of wording and will assist the Commission in advising the charity in the future. The alterations should not be adopted, however, unless the proposed charity trustees understand and are entirely happy with them.

2.3.6   Registration number

Once the Charity Commission have accepted a proposed charity for registration a registration number will be allocated to the charity. This should be recorded since it will need to be quoted in future correspondence with both the Commission and HMRC. In addition, many charities like to quote the registration number on their fundraising literature and other documents. A copy of the governing instrument should be given to every trustee and senior officer of the charity and the original should be kept in a safe place, such as a bank.

2.3.7   Significance of registration

The significance of registration is that it provides conclusive proof that the charity is legally a charity and has complied with the legal obligation to register. This does not mean that it is necessarily well run, although the Charity Commission's monitoring activities (which are still being developed) are designed to provide an assurance that there is a degree of supervision applicable, at least to larger charities. If a charity is, for any reason, not registered, the this does not signify that it is *not* a charity, since charitable status depends on the purposes of the organisation rather than any specific formality. A charity which should be registered, but by some oversight has not been registered, can be registered late, but the trustees may be asked to send the Commission more information, including accounts, than is required for a proposed charity.

Anyone may apply to the Commission for a copy of the governing instrument, statements of account and other details concerning a registered charity. The basic information is kept on computer and indicates whether the charity concerned has complied with its statutory obligations. Registration underlines the fact that a charity is a public trust, for which the charity trustees are accountable.

Every registered charity with an gross income (ie receipts) of £10,000 or more in its last financial year must state the fact that it is registered on all its official documents, including cheques, invoices and fundraising literature.

2.4   REGISTRATION IN SCOTLAND

In place of a system of registration, HMRC maintains an index of recognised bodies and itself examines the governing instrument of any body seeking charitable tax relief. The relevant office is the Edinburgh branch of FICO.

If HMRC is satisfied from scrutiny of the governing instrument that the body concerned is exclusively charitable it will allocate an index number and send a letter of confirmation which the body may use as evidence of its charitable status. Anyone may obtain from HMRC the name and address of a recognised body but there is a statutory obligation on the body itself (rather than HMRC) to supply a copy of its governing instrument – at a reasonable charge – to any enquirer.

2.5   CHANGING THE CONSTITUTION

Practical experience in administering a charity, or changes in its resources, in the relevant law or in the circumstances of the beneficiaries, or more general changes in society, may convince the trustees that the governing instrument needs to be altered or updated. In extreme cases, the purpose of the charity may no longer provide a sensible use for its assets. It is one of the principles of charity law that, if necessary, and provided that the correct procedure is carried out, the purposes or other provisions of a charity's governing instrument may be altered. In fact, it is the trustees' legal duty to take steps to introduce change, where this is necessary in order to make effective use of the charity's resources.

If it appears that an alteration is needed, it is often wise first to double check that an unduly restrictive interpretation of the existing document has not been adopted. Sometimes trustees will be advised that there already exists an implied power to use the charity's resources for the new activity which they have in mind.

If a more liberal interpretation will not assist, or would strain the language of the governing instrument, the next question is whether there is a specific power to alter the instrument.

2.5.1   Alteration to memorandum and articles of association

There is a power to alter the memorandum and articles of association of a charitable company, but if a change to the objects clause in the memorandum (or to any provision in the articles which governs the use of the charity's assets) is envisaged then, in the case of a charity in England and Wales, the Charity Commission's consent will be needed in advance and it will be necessary to follow the procedures of company law to effect the required change. Failure to lodge the Commission's consent constitutes an offence under company law.

The Commission are unlikely to give their consent without good reason and will normally expect the new purposes to be akin to the original purposes. A fundamental change, for example to assist old people instead of children or vice versa, or to benefit the inhabitants of a completely different geographical area, is not likely to be accepted by the Commission, without at least negotiating some special arrangement to keep any existing assets available for the old purposes.

In the case of a Scottish charitable company, it is necessary to obtain clearance from HMRC before making the alteration.

2.5.2 Express power of alteration

There is often an express power of alteration in the constitution of an unincorporated charitable association. If such a power exists the procedures must be followed meticulously. This generally means notifying the members in advance and calling a general meeting. If a change in the purposes is envisaged, it is wise to consult the Charity Commission (or, in Scotland, HMRC) well in advance, even where the constitution does not specifically require this. The same applies in the case of a declaration of trust which contains an express power of alteration.

2.5.3 Alternative procedures

If the governing instrument does not contain a power of alteration, or if the power in question does not extend to the sort of alteration envisaged (for example, where it specifically excludes a change in the purposes of the charity) and the trustees are convinced that the purposes should be altered, there are two alternative procedures, depending on the size of the charity.

2.5.3.1 Statutory power

If the annual income of the charity does not exceed £5,000 the trustees have a statutory power to pass a resolution (by a two-thirds majority) to alter the charity's purposes or administrative provisions. The terms of the resolution must be sent to the Charity Commission (in England and Wales) and a notice of concurrence must be received from them before the change can take place. The trustees should advertise their proposals and seek comments from the public, but the method of doing so is for them to decide. Any new purposes must be akin to the original purposes.

2.5.3.2 Scheme

In other cases, it will be necessary to apply to the Charity Commission (or, in Scotland, the Inner House of the Court of Session) for a 'scheme'. A scheme is a legal document, equivalent to a court order, which modifies or replaces the existing governing instrument. Many older charities are now governed entirely by a scheme or series of schemes. The Commission have considerable experience of making schemes and have developed an extensive body of precedents. The procedure in England and Wales is as follows.

2.5.3.2.1 Procedure

The trustees should first write to the Charity Commission, or seek an interview, to explain the difficulties in administering the charity under its present governing instrument, identifying every difficulty. They should be ready with their ideas for a more workable arrangement but be prepared to consider alternatives which the Commission, from their experience of similar situations, may suggest. Once the Commission are satisfied of the need for a scheme and have agreed on what it is broadly to achieve, they will invite the trustees to make a formal application. Once made, such an application cannot be withdrawn unless the Commission agree.

The Commission will then prepare a draft scheme for the trustees to consider. When any necessary modifications have been made to the draft, the trustees are required to arrange the publication of notices which may be posted in the area of benefit in the case of a local charity or published in a suitable newspaper or journal, inviting members of the public to put forward objections or suggestions to the Commission. If the proposals are controversial the proposed scheme may have to be modified or even abandoned, or the Commission may decide that any scheme should be made by the High Court. In view of this, it is prudent for the trustees to identify and deal with potential objections to a scheme before publication of the notices.

Assuming that there are no objections (which is usually the case) or that the objections can be overcome, the Commission will seal the new scheme, thus bringing it into effect, once they have received evidence of publication from the trustees.

The remaining step is the publication of final notices to the effect that the scheme has been established, which sets the time-limit for the (rare) procedure of appealing against the scheme to the High Court.

The trustees will not need professional advice concerning the establishment of a scheme unless the Commission require them to obtain it (for example, where the trustees are seeking wider powers of investment) or, in some cases, the trustees have specific proposals of their own and wish to formulate them in detail, rather than simply relying on the Commission's recommendations.

Nowadays, a scheme will often contain an express power to vary the administrative provisions. This results from a change of policy by the Commission in 1995.

2.5.3.2.2   Cy-près doctrine

A scheme may either alter the administrative arrangements of the charity, for example by changing the composition of the body of trustees, or it may alter the purposes of the charity, or both. Where the purposes are to be altered the Commission are bound by the cy-près doctrine, a Norman-French expression which goes back to the fourteenth century and means 'close to' or 'akin to'. The existence of this doctrine is one of the reasons why some charities have survived for hundreds of years and still perform a useful and relevant function. It requires the Commission (or the court), when altering the purposes of a charity, to keep as close as reasonably practicable to the original purpose, to respect the spirit of the original gift and, as far as possible, to respect the intention of the founder of the charity. It is, therefore, a protection for, and encouragement to, the founders of charities and those who subsequently make gifts to them. A good cy-près scheme will enlarge the discretion of the trustees by not being too specific about the method of fulfilling the charity's purpose, thus enabling the charity to adapt to future changes in the surrounding circumstances.

2.5.4   Reviewing aims and procedures

As a general rule, it is a good idea for trustees to give serious consideration to a charity's purposes, administrative provisions and general direction at least once in every generation, and more frequently when the charity is operating in a rapidly changing field. In addition, changes in local government or health service administration or in recommended methods of treatment, changes in local or central government provision or grant-making policies, or the establishment of other organisations operating in the same field, can all provide specific reasons to consider change.

2.5.5   The new governing instrument

Once a charity's governing instrument has been altered or replaced the trustees have a duty to supply the Charity Commission (or, in Scotland, HMRC) promptly with a copy of the new document, unless (in England

and Wales) it is a scheme made by the Commission themselves (in which case they will have a copy already). The original of the new document should be kept in a safe place, with the earlier documents, and a copy should be supplied to each of the trustees and senior officers.

2.6 AMALGAMATION

It may be desirable to amalgamate two or more charities which have compatible purposes, in order to achieve synergy, including economies of scale, and to avoid duplication of effort. There are various practical questions which must be resolved, for example who will be trustees, whether all existing staff will continue to be employed, what the name of the new charity will be and where it will have its headquarters, etc. Serious consideration of these matters must be undertaken and adequate time and discussion should be allowed to find the best available solution. It is also important that one body which is taking on the functions of another should carry out careful checks to ensure that there are no hidden problems – either financial or legal – in its past administration.

2.6.1 Transfer of assets

There are several possible legal methods of achieving amalgamation, depending on the original governing instruments. The simplest method is for one charity to wind up under a power contained in its constitution and transfer its assets over to another charity, which may, or may not, effect some alteration in its name or governing instrument as a consequence. This may give rise to difficulties, however, if, for example, the charity which has been wound up has been left a legacy or is entitled to payments under covenant.

A more tactful method of achieving amalgamation is to set up a new charity incorporating elements from the original charities, which then wind up and transfer their assets to the new charity. The same problem regarding legacies can, of course, arise, but this may be avoided if the new constitution expressly indicates that it is an amalgamation of the existing charities, and identifies them.

Where this arrangement is not constitutionally possible owing to the absence of a power to wind up (or an absence of a power to make an alteration which can legally enable a power to wind up to be adopted) there are two methods of achieving an amalgamation, depending on the size of the charity.

2.6.1.1 *Statutory power*

If a charity's annual income does not exceed £5,000 and the charity does not hold land which is used for charitable purposes, the trustees are permitted, by statute, to pass a resolution (by a two-thirds majority) to transfer the assets to another charity having similar objectives. They may then give public notice of the proposal, notify the Charity Commission, and obtain a notice of concurrence (in England and Wales) and put the transfer into effect. Once the charity's assets have been transferred, the trustees of the transferring charity should send the final statement of account to the Commission (in Scotland, to HMRC) with a request that the charity should be removed from the Register of Charities.

The transferee charity needs to pass a resolution to accept the transfer and any funds which were permanent endowment originally remain so after the transfer.

2.6.1.2   Scheme

In other cases the appropriate procedure will be to apply to the Charity Commission (or in Scotland, the Court of Session) for a scheme, which may either simply authorise the transfer of assets or, if the situation requires more elaborate arrangements, take the form of a cy-près scheme formally providing for the charities concerned to 'be administered as one charity'. The cy-près procedure enables the original charities to continue to exist in a technical sense, so that the new combined charity is, thus, entitled to any covenanted payments or legacies to which the original charities are, or may become, entitled.

2.7   WINDING UP

Some charities continue indefinitely; others, such as appeal funds, have a limited lifespan from the outset and cease to exist once their purposes have been achieved and their assets have been used. In other cases a charity may be brought to an end deliberately, either in the course of a de facto amalgamation, or to replace an existing, unincorporated association with a charitable company. A charity may also be brought to an end because it has ceased to be financially viable or to perform a useful function.

A charitable company may be wound up. It ought to be wound up (or at least should cease to operate) if it becomes insolvent, ie if its assets will not cover its liabilities. The memorandum of association will normally state that any assets remaining after all liabilities have been met should be transferred to another charity having similar objectives or, failing that, should be applied for some other charitable purpose. It is wise to attempt to find a recipient charity which is carrying on work which the defunct charity would have supported if it had been able to do so, and to ensure that the recipient charity is registered (if it is liable to be registered) and is up to date with its accounts. If the remaining assets are sufficient, or if the purposes to be supported are being carried on by different charities, there may be more than one recipient.

There is no reason why a recipient charity should not be a charity which is administered by one or more of the charity trustees of the defunct charity, provided, of course, that the purpose of the recipient charity is similar. That should not, however, be the only reason for choosing that recipient. The trustees retain, to the end, their fiduciary duty to apply the charitable funds conscientiously for the purpose for which they were contributed, and must be prepared to justify their decisions on objective grounds.

2.7.1   Express power to wind up

In the case of a charitable unincorporated association or a modern declaration of trust, it is usual to find an express power to wind up and a direction to apply the remaining assets (if any) for similar charitable purposes. If there is no power of dissolution, but there is a power of amendment which is not expressly restricted, it may be possible legally to adopt an amendment to the constitution which confers a power of dissolution. It is advisable to consult the Charity Commission, HMRC (in Scotland) or an independent legal adviser before doing so, to ensure that the power is properly exercised and cannot be challenged at a later date.

Once a charity in England and Wales has been dissolved and its remaining assets transferred, the last trustees should write to the Commission with a copy of the final statement of account, showing that no assets remain, and ask the Commission to remove the charity from the register. The Commission are bound to remove any charity which has ceased to exist or to operate and will not re-allocate the registration number but keep a record of it.

In the case of a charity in Scotland, HMRC should be sent a copy of the final statement of account and informed of the dissolution.

2.7.2   Statutory power

Where a charity is governed by declaration of trust or by a scheme, there may be no power of dissolution or amendment. If, particularly in the case of an older trust or a charity governed by a scheme, there is any permanent capital (technically called 'permanent endowment', meaning that the charity has the use of the income but must preserve the capital) there will generally be no power to wind up the charity. However, there is such a power if the charity's gross income in the last financial year was no more than £1,000 and none of its permanent endowment consists of land. In the case of a very small, permanently endowed charity in this category, there is a statutory power to pass a resolution enabling the permanent endowment capital to be treated as income (and thus spent), provided that there is no suitable charity to which the assets can instead be transferred, that public notice of the proposal is given and that (in England and Wales) the Charity Commission's notice of concurrence is obtained or that (in Scotland) the Lord Advocate is notified.

2.7.3 Scheme

In all other cases, if the charity ceases to be viable or effective the only practicable solution is to apply to the Charity Commission (or, in Scotland, the Court of Session) for a scheme to make some workable provision for the application of the income. In this way, charities which were originally engaged in their own specific activities, such as running a school or a group of almshouses, which eventually became unworkable or uneconomic, may eventually be transformed into grant-making trusts or amalgamated with larger institutions. In this way, they continue to be useful and to contribute to the main purpose which the founder intended.

2.7.4 Powers of Commission or Court of Session to wind up

Finally, it must be pointed out that if the trustees of a charity misapply its assets the Charity Commission will not remove its charitable status. There are various remedial steps open to them, one of which is to order the transfer of the charity's assets to another charity and the winding up of the abused charity. This may be accompanied by taking proceedings against the trustees for breach of trust. In Scotland, similar steps can be taken by the Court of Session on the application of the Lord Advocate.

2.8 CY-PRÈS SCHEMES – EXAMPLES

The following examples illustrate schemes which have been made, or on which decisions have been taken, where the original purposes of the charities were no longer viable:

(1) Roman's bequest for games which would have been illegal: memorial to testator in some other way (circa AD300).

(2) Surplus almshouse land: used for school (eighteenth century).

(3) Trust to maintain bishopric in America: trust to maintain bishopric in Canada (nineteenth century).

(4) Elizabethan charity for the redemption of captives of the Barbary pirates: trust for educational purposes (nineteenth century).

(5) Ancient charities for prisons: trust for relief of poverty (nineteenth century).

(6)   Ancient charity for boys out of control: boys' public school (nineteenth century).

(7)   Historic almshouse building no longer required for housing purposes: museum (1961).

(8)   Charity to relieve the poor rate: trust to benefit inhabitants generally (1971).

(9)   Trust to provide eleven barrels of white herrings and eight barrels of red herrings to the poor of a fishing village: trust for relief of need in the area (1973).

(10) Teetotal village hall: alcoholic drinks permitted (1975).

(11) Hospital which closed: grant-making trust to relieve the sick (1976).

(12) Appeal fund to provide village hall (never built) to commemorate the Coronation: provision of a public clock and garden to commemorate the Queen's Silver Jubilee (1977).

(13) Ancient charity to give loans to young men: trust for education and advancement in life for young people (1988).

(14) Elizabethan charity to maintain trunk road through London: trust to benefit inhabitants of relevant boroughs (1989).

(15) Old charities to provide grazing rights for freemen of borough and their widows: trust for benefit of all the inhabitants (1993).

CHAPTER 3

MONEY AND PROPERTY

3.1   ACCOUNTING

It is clear that anyone who controls public money should keep a careful record of it and be accountable to the public for its use. Whatever other economies are adopted, the area of financial control and accountability should not be skimped, even if this involves expenditure which does not directly further the charity's purposes.

3.2   ACCOUNTS AND RECORD-KEEPING

The requirements are intended to apply to all charities with the main objective being to improve the quality of financial reporting while at the same time reducing the options for accounting practice and presentation.

Systems must therefore be set up to ensure that the charity complies. In England and Wales records must be kept for at least six years, and for registered charities, and those which should be registered, the annual report and accounts are required to be submitted to the Charity Commission within 10 months of the end of the charity's financial year. Scottish charities, to which different rules apply, and other charities must be able to produce their annual accounts etc on request within the same timescale.

3.2.1   Structure

The detailed accounting requirements are contained in the Statement of Recommended Practice ('SORP') issued by the Charity Commission and approved by the Accounting Standards Board.

The accounts of a charity (other than a small charity) should comprise the following:

(1)   a statement of financial activities;

(2)   if a charitable company, a summary income and expenditure account (to comply with the Companies Act 1985);

(3)   a balance sheet;

(4)   where required by other accounting standards, a cashflow statement;

(5)   notes analysing figures in the accounts and notes explaining the accounting policies adopted.

In Scotland, a charity is required to prepare an income and expenditure account instead of the statement of financial activities but, in the case of a charitable company, a summary statement of financial activities must be prepared instead of a summary income and expenditure account.

In all accounts, corresponding figures for the previous accounting period should be given and the period covered by the accounts should also be shown.

3.2.2   Small charities

A charity which is not a limited company and whose annual income does not exceed the threshold set by the regulations (currently £100,000) is treated as a small charity and is permitted to prepare simplified accounts etc. In Scotland, the current 'small' limit is only £25,000 and this applies to all receipts, not only income.

Unless specified otherwise in the governing document, such small charities should prepare:

(1)   an annual report;

(2)   a receipts and payments account;

(3)   a statement of assets and liabilities (England and Wales), or a statement of balances (Scotland);

(4)   notes of any material matters not mentioned in the annual report.

It is worth noting that because only receipts and payments are disclosed, a 'true and fair view' is not required or given and therefore the fundamental accounting concepts of *going concern, accruals* and *prudence* cannot apply.

The only such concept which does apply is *consistency.*

Where a charity's 'small' status alters from one year to the next, necessitating a switch from receipts and payments to full accounts or vice versa, the corresponding amounts for the previous year should be restated on the basis of the new presentation.

3.2.3   Formats

The financial statements must be presented in a form which follows the regulations and SORP. Certain headings and their layout are prescribed, for example incoming resources or direct charitable expenditure. Any headings may be expanded as appropriate to the circumstances, but should not be excessively detailed. The notes to the accounts can be used to amplify the information in both numeric and narrative form. Further narrative information can be given in the annual report (see below).

The SORP deals in some detail with the treatment of various types of income and expenditure. Netting off of one against the other is generally not acceptable, although in some cases this may be unavoidable. If so, then an estimate of the relevant gross figures (if material) should be given.

The requirements closely follow company legislation and therefore the notes to the accounts are required to show, inter alia, details of:

(1)   transactions with trustees and related charities;

(2)   trustees' indemnity insurance;

(3)   employees' emoluments;

(4)   audit costs.

The layout and content of the balance sheet and cash flow statement are also prescribed. In general, these too follow the Companies Act 1985 presentation and should also comply with relevant accounting standards.

Appendix G gives illustrative examples of the statement of financial activities together with explanatory notes.

3.2.4   Policies

Specific guidance is also available on best practice in respect of a number of areas affecting the accounts. These include the requirement to follow normal accounting standards, disclosure of the accounting policies adopted, and, in detail, the accounting treatment for different kinds of funds (for example restricted and unrestricted funds, permanent endowment funds and designated funds) as well as the reconciliation and movements on the funds.

3.2.5   The annual report

In addition to the accounts of the charity, trustees are also required to prepare a separate document known as the annual report in respect of each financial year.

This report should provide certain legal and administrative information such as the nature of the founding deed and a list of the trustees who have served during the year. The report must also set out the charity's main aims and objectives and how they are to be achieved. It should be sufficiently informative to enable the reader to understand the operations of the charity and should show clearly:

(1)   the policies of the charity;

(2)   a review of developments, activities and achievements;

(3)   a review of the financial position, including a review of specific funds if necessary.

These requirements are similar to those for a directors' report for a company. The preparation of the annual report and financial statements is the responsibility of *all* the trustees and, therefore, the charity's administrative procedures should be such that a draft of these documents is exhibited to all trustees in advance of the meeting at which they are to be approved. Subsequently, the report and accounts should be signed on behalf of the trustees in accordance with any existing arrangements for financial delegation.

3.2.6   Branches

One area which often leads to confusion is the treatment of branches in the accounts of the charity. A branch can sometimes be known by another name such as 'supporters' group', 'friends of ...' and so on.

Branches are defined as entities or administrative bodies set up, for example, to conduct a particular aspect of the business of the main charity or to conduct the business of the main charity in a particular geographical area. They may or may not be legal entities which are separate from the main charity. It is a matter of law whether a branch is a legal entity in its own right.

It is normal for a charity to use branches in different ways, usually for fundraising, and it can be argued that any money raised in the name of the charity must belong to it. However, branches should only be included in the accounts of the charity if they are under its control. A group of friends, for example, who raise funds for the charity but are not themselves undertaking charitable activities would not constitute a branch.

A branch usually has most of the following characteristics:

(1)   it uses the name of the main charity in its title;

(2)   it raises funds exclusively for the charity, for use either at head office or local level;

(3)   it uses the registration number of the main charity to obtain tax relief;

(4)   it is perceived by the public to be a branch of the charity;

(5)   the main charity supports it with material, publicity, staff funding etc.

3.3   INDEPENDENT AUDIT

In general, smaller charities are required to have their accounts examined by an independent person (not necessarily a qualified accountant) with relevant financial expertise. Larger charities must have a professional audit.

The question whether a particular charity must be audited is determined initially by the governing document. If that says the accounts are to be audited, then they must be   irrespective of the size of the charity.

It is common to use the word 'audit' in such documents, especially those drawn up prior to the regulation of the auditing profession in 1991. If it was not the intention to have a professional 'audit' carried out, and the size of the charity permits, then the document may be interpreted as requiring no more than an independent examination. Otherwise, an amendment may be sensible.

After looking at the document, the next question to be considered is whether the charity is a company. If it is, then it is exempt from audit if annual income does not exceed £90,000; it requires an independent examiner's report if annual income is between £90,001 and £250,000; and only if income exceeds £250,000 is a full audit required. A full audit would also be required where the charity's balance sheet total exceeded £1.4m even if the income did not exceed the above limits. The exemptions apply to stand-alone companies only and therefore exclude parent companies and subsidiaries.

Note also that for charities with income between £10,000 and £100,000 pa, there is an option to apply the receipts and payments basis rather than the accruals concept and a 'true and fair' view is not then required. See the comments on small charities at 3.2.2 above.

If the charity is not a company, it is exempt from audit or independent examination if the annual income does not exceed £10,000 (but not for Scottish charities); an independent examiner's report is required if the income is up to £250,000 (£100,000 for Scottish charities); and it is only if either the income or expenditure in either of the two previous financial years exceeds £250,000 (£100,000 for Scottish charities) that a full audit is required.

3.4 TAX AND RATES

Apart from the council tax, which applies to domestic property, and VAT, where, despite constant campaigning by charities, the reliefs are piecemeal and highly specialised, charities and those people who give to charities benefit from generous and long-standing reliefs from tax. Charities also benefit from relief from non-domestic rates. It has been said that the reason for this generosity is that charities were performing public service tasks before taxation (and certainly before income tax) was introduced; taxing charities would, therefore, benefit no one. Be that as it may, the existence of tax reliefs is a strong, motivating factor for those contemplating setting up or supporting a charity and it is open to any individual taxpayer to avoid paying tax by making (larger) charitable contributions instead.

3.4.1 Income and capital gains

No charity should pay tax on its income or capital gains. Relief is available, as of right, on receipts from all sources except trading (other than trading in direct furtherance of the charity's main purpose or by beneficiaries of the charity), provided that the receipts are used or applied for charitable purposes or for one of the ancillary purposes (such as 'qualifying expenditure' or a 'qualifying investment') recognised by statute. Trading which does not directly further the charity's purposes (for example the selling of Bibles by a religious charity), is incapable of being a charitable purpose in itself, and an investment or item of expenditure which falls outside the category of 'qualifying' expenditure will rarely occur and scarcely ever be necessary. Where tax, for example corporation tax on company dividends, is deducted at source, the charity should promptly claim repayment from HM Revenue and Customs ('HMRC').

3.4.2 Property used for charitable purposes

A charity in rateable occupation of land and buildings is entitled, as of right, to 80% relief from non-domestic rates on property used wholly or mainly for charitable purposes, or for fundraising. In addition, the local authority has a discretion to grant further relief up to 100%, although this must generally be applied for, and justified, every year.

3.4.3 Payments from supporters

Where a supporter gives a charity a sum of at least £250 (the current lower limit for 'gift aid') or makes a deed of covenant in its favour to pay an annual sum of any amount for at least three years, both supporter (if a higher rate taxpayer) and charity benefit. The payment is tax-deductible and the charity is entitled to claim from HMRC the amount of tax for which the supporter would have been liable if the payment had not been made to the charity. (For a suggested form of deed of covenant, see Appendix A.)

3.4.4 Payroll Deduction Scheme

Under the Payroll Deduction Scheme, an employee whose employer participates in the Scheme is able to make automatic tax-deductible gifts from his or her earnings to an agency charity, which may then reclaim the notional tax.

3.4.5 Gifts

Gifts to charity which would otherwise attract capital gains tax or inheritance tax are exempt, but there is no additional benefit from HMRC for the charity. This situation arises where a gift of land, chattels or investments is made to a charity by will or during the donor's lifetime.

3.4.6 HM Revenue and Customs guidance

The Financial Intermediaries and Claims Office ('FICO') of HMRC produces some very helpful guidance, as well as official forms, for use by charities and their supporters. It is recognised generally that gifts to charity should be encouraged and that charities should be encouraged to take advantage of the tax reliefs available to them. Indeed, trustees could be held liable for a breach of trust if they cause the charity an actual or notional loss by failing to take advantage of the available tax reliefs. In complex cases, where the situation is not covered by HMRC forms or guidance, professional advice from a lawyer or accountant will be desirable.

3.5 INSURANCE

3.5.1 Fire, other damage and theft

Charity trustees should insure property belonging to the charity against the usual risks such as fire, other damage and theft. Although the basic rule of English trust law is that trustees may insure property up to two-thirds of its value, it has been recognised for many years that in the case of charities, full re-instatement value is appropriate if this is possible. Certain charities whose assets, including major works of art, are irreplaceable, have chosen, as a matter of policy, to protect those assets in some other way, such as stringent security precautions, and not to insure. Whilst security precautions which are consistent with the purposes of the charity are prudent and may, indeed, help to reduce the premium payable, it is only in the most exceptional cases and after full consideration of all the implications that a body of charity trustees will escape criticism if it decides not to insure the charity's property. For the great majority of charities, such insurance is essential.

3.5.2 Vandalism and terrorism

Charities with buildings in vulnerable places must now consider insurance against the risk of deliberate damage from vandalism and terrorism.

3.5.3 Public and employer's liability

Insurance is also required against the risk of public liability and employer's liability. Failure to insure against these risks renders the trustees potentially liable on a personal basis, if the charity is unincorporated.

3.5.4 Fidelity insurance

A connected issue is fidelity insurance, where an agent or employee of the charity has, in practice, to be given a large measure of responsibility and cannot be supervised constantly by the trustees.

3.5.5 Particular risks

In some circumstances, it may be desirable to take out specific insurance against a particular risk on an ad hoc or short-term basis. For example, insurance might be needed if the charity has received a legacy which it plans to spend, but there is a chance that a relative or dependant of the deceased can make a successful claim under the Inheritance (Provision for Family and Dependants) Act 1975.

3.5.6 Liability insurance

A relatively new area of insurance which can provide additional protection for charity trustees in certain cases, is liability insurance. This insurance protects a trustee against the possibility of having to personally meet a liability arising from a breach of trust, or breach of duty towards the charity (except a wilful or reckless breach of duty). Trustees may always insure themselves, at their own expense, against such liability, but in some cases there may be justification for the charity to pay the premium. The payment of such a premium amounts to a benefit to the trustee who is covered and, therefore, is not permitted, unless it is authorised by the Charity Commission (or the court) or specifically provided for in the charity's constitution. The kind of situation in which the Commission are likely to be sympathetic to a proposed change in a charity's governing instrument in order to permit such a payment, or an application for a special order to authorise it, is where there is some exceptionally serious risk of liability or where the liability itself could be very great, and it can be demonstrated that it may be difficult to find trustees if the cover cannot be provided at the charity's expense.

3.5.7 Other means of financial protection

In cases where insurance cannot be obtained by the charity there are other methods of obtaining financial protection. In some cases, a person or body other than the charity will have an insurable interest in the subject matter, for example where a painting or sculpture is lent by a charity to a museum or gallery, which itself undertakes to insure it. In other cases, such as where the risk in question is a commercial risk, it may be necessary to consider setting up a limited liability company, which may not itself be a charity, to carry out the activity which gives rise to the risk. This arrangement is common where a charity wishes to raise money through some trading activity (see 'Trading' at **3.12** below).

3.6 INVESTMENT

Charity money which is not due to be spent in the near future should be working for the charity. Funds which will be required within a short time should be placed on deposit at a recognised bank or building society, or some other short-term arrangement should be made to preserve them safely.

Where it is known that funds will not be required for some time, and it is possible to calculate the amount which will then be needed, it is worth considering investment in a short-dated government stock or some other short-term investment. It is sometimes possible to achieve capital growth in this way by careful planning and timing.

In the case of permanent endowment or capital funds which are unlikely to be required for several years ahead, the trustees are able to take a longer view and consider specifically not only the charity's need for income but also the desirability of achieving capital growth. Generally, growth is most likely to be obtained by investing in unit trusts, shares in companies or land and buildings, and by being in a position to leave the funds in an invested state until the time for disposing of the investments is ripe.

3.6.1 Common investment funds

A sensible choice for many bodies of trustees in England and Wales is to invest in a common investment fund ('CIF'), which is itself a charity and is established exclusively for the investment of charity funds. A CIF operates in a similar way to an investment trust but is able to pay its dividends gross. Common deposit funds ('CDFs') are similarly available to charities. Several new CIFs have been set up in recent years and the Charity Commission will supply a list on request.

A new development has been the creation of 'ethical' CIFs which are particularly designed for charities whose objects (for example the promotion of temperance) render certain types of investments (such as shares in distilleries) peculiarly unsuitable.

3.6.2   Powers of investment

Modern governing instruments nearly always contain unrestricted investment powers, enabling the trustees to choose any form of investment, whether in the UK or abroad. Normally, however, trustees should avoid the acquisition of property which does not produce any income or which is in any way speculative, including an unsecured loan, since such a choice is not compatible with the trustees' role of obtaining income to use for the charity's purposes, while protecting the charity's assets. Investment abroad can produce practical difficulties, for example in undertaking transactions from a distance and keeping a close watch on the relevant market. Traded options and unquoted investments can be dangerous unless expert advice is obtained. Some more traditional forms of investment can also be imprudent, such as the purchase of undated stocks, loans on the mortgage of property, partly paid shares, or deferred or non-voting shares.

3.6.2.1   *Statutory powers (unincorporated charities)*

Where there is no express power of investment in the governing instrument, the trustees are limited to the statutory powers. There are now statutory powers of investment for unincorporated charities in England and Wales arising from the Trustee Act 2000. In addition there are specific statutory duties for trustees.

3.6.2.2   *Schemes*

In the case of substantial charities in England and Wales having invested funds of £1m or more, the Charity Commission have in recent years been prepared to make schemes widening or updating the investment powers so as to confer a greater discretion on the trustees. This kind of scheme is not, generally, available unless the trustees have a reasonable track record of investment success and can produce professional advice to the effect that the charity would benefit from wider powers. The need for such schemes is likely to decrease considerably with the new legislation.

3.6.3 Advice on investments

The law requires trustees to obtain advice on all investment decisions, except for the simplest and most traditional forms of investment. Trustees should bear in mind the desirability of spreading their funds between a number of investments, rather than keeping all their eggs in one basket. It is essential that the trustees should obtain advice from a stockbroker, merchant banker or other reputable financial adviser who has substantial experience and is either registered or exempt from registration under the Financial Services Act 1986. It is desirable to obtain such advice and to instruct the adviser to keep the charity's investments under review, even where the trustees themselves include someone with relevant experience.

3.6.3.1 *Investment advisers*

In some cases, particularly larger charities, the trustees will not be in a position personally to manage the charity's investment portfolio. It may, therefore, be wise to appoint either an investment advisor or some other expert to undertake this task and delegate the power to acquire and dispose of investments to that person or firm. It is now considered essential that trustees should have an express power in the governing instrument to delegate the management of investments, and it may therefore be necessary either to make an alteration to the charity's governing instrument for this purpose, or, if there is no power of alteration, to apply for a scheme or order conferring the necessary power. In exercising such a power, the trustees should have regular meetings with the experts, set the investment policy under a written agreement, confine the expert strictly to the charity's legal powers of investment, receive prompt and regular reports of all transactions, reserve the power to cancel the arrangement at any time, and review it every two years. It is often desirable to include an express power to appoint a nominee company to hold the investments on the charity's behalf.

3.6.4 Holding of investments

The normal rule is that the investments should be held in the name of the charity or the trustee body, if incorporated, or in the names of the individual trustees. It is not, of course, convenient for the investments to be held by a number of individual trustees in the long term, since trustees change and records, therefore, have to be updated in order to avoid difficulties later.

In some cases, the use of a corporate nominee may be considered: it is advisable to ensure that the charity's governing instrument contains an express provision enabling a nominee to be used for the purpose. Where there is scope for a two-tier governing body, it is often convenient to appoint a trust corporation or other more or less permanent body to hold the investments safely for the charity whilst the day-to-day investment and other management decisions are taken by the more rapidly changing body of charity trustees. Where this system has been set up formally, the holding body, if it is a trust corporation, may be designated the custodian trustee and the charity trustees designated the managing trustees.

3.6.4.1   *Incorporation*

A two-tier structure is not always desirable, particularly if there is likely to be a good deal of movement in the funds. In England and Wales, if the charity is not itself incorporated it may be wise to consider incorporation of the trustee body under the Charities Act 1993. By this procedure, which involves an application to the Charity Commission for a certificate of incorporation, the trustee body is given a name and legal personality of its own. This can bring considerable administrative benefits, not least in the holding of investments, as well as incidentally protecting the trustees from personal liability towards outside parties. An alternative, which may be appropriate in the case of a Scottish charity, would be to set up a limited liability company and seek (if necessary by order of the Commission) its appointment as trustee of the charity, the effect of such order being to constitute the company as a trust corporation for the purposes of that charity only.

3.6.5   Land investment

An amendment to the law has been recommended, but at present land is not an authorised investment for charities. Some charities have power to invest in land, which may be an express power or a power implied from the fact that the charity already holds land as an investment. The Charity Commission may also make an ad hoc order authorising a charity in England or Wales to purchase land as an investment, if the Commission are provided with evidence, in the shape of a report from a qualified surveyor, which demonstrates that the proposed investment is in the charity's interests. (See further 'Land and buildings' below.)

3.7   LAND AND BUILDINGS

Buildings (except caravans and other removable structures) legally form part of the land on which they are built. Therefore, for convenience, wherever 'land' is referred to in this book, any buildings on the land are included in that expression.

Charities own land for two main purposes: as an income-producing investment or for their own use. It is worth noting that, judging by past history, land has performed as a better long-term investment for charities than any other investment. The endowments of very old, established charities which are well-endowed today all consisted of land, some of which was of very little value at the outset. Functional land includes almshouses, village halls, recreation grounds, art galleries, museums, places of worship, church halls, schools, hospitals, hostels, swimming pools, historic monuments, archaeological sites, community centres, leisure centres, libraries, women's refuges and the administrative offices of charities.

Land may be owned outright, leased, rented or hired. Where the charity is the owner of land, the trustees are subject to a number of responsibilities as property-owners. They are obliged to make arrangements for repairs and insurance to the extent that these duties are not undertaken by anyone else. In addition, where they occupy land they are liable for non-domestic rates and water bills.

In the case of leasehold or rented land, charities will be responsible for paying the rent and observing the covenants in the lease. In Scotland there may be feu duties or other incidents.

3.7.1 Holding of land

Title to land is normally held in the name of the charity or the trustee body, if incorporated, or in the name of a custodian trustee, or in the names of the individual trustees, where neither the charity nor the trustee body is incorporated and there is no custodian or corporate holding trustee.

If individual trustees hold the land there is no upper limit on their number (as there would be with a private trust), but there must be at least two individual trustees in order to give a valid receipt for capital money, ie to be able to sell, mortgage or exchange the land or grant a lease at a premium. This immediately gives rise to the problem that unless every new trustee is appointed by deed and amendments are made to the particulars kept at the Land Registry (if the land is registered), the title will be vested in a dwindling number of individuals, some of whom may cease to be trustees, and technical problems may arise when it is necessary, at some future date, to prove the charity's ownership.

This problem can be overcome by one of two methods, outlined below.

3.7.1.1 Certificate of incorporation (England and Wales)

When the land is held on a short lease, or it is expected that there will be frequent transactions, as where land is held as an investment and leases will need to be granted or enforced from time to time, or where the land is likely to be sold, it is appropriate to consider applying to the Charity Commission for a certificate of incorporation under the Charities Act 1993 (see 'Incorporation' at 3.6.4.1 above). Alternatively, and in Scotland (where incorporation of the trustees by certificate is not available), it may be considered wise to set up a limited liability company to be appointed as the trustee, or holding trustee, of the charity.

3.7.1.2 *Land vested in the Official Custodian (England and Wales)*

In cases where the land is likely to be held for many years to come, for example where it constitutes a permanent endowment of the charity and is used for its charitable purposes, the ideal solution is to apply to the Charity Commission for an order vesting title to the land in the Official Custodian for Charities. In some cases, assistance from the charity's legal adviser may be necessary. The Official Custodian then, technically, holds the title and in the case of registered land is recorded as the proprietor at the Land Registry, but has no personal responsibilities and powers of management. All powers and responsibilities remain with the charity trustees, who are entitled to enter into agreements or take proceedings relating to the land in the name of the Official Custodian.

3.7.2   Sale, exchange or leasing of land (England and Wales)

Before 31 December 1992, charities were frequently required to obtain the Charity Commission's consent, or an order excepting the charity from the requirement to obtain consent, to the sale, exchange or leasing of land. Under the system which has operated since then, the transaction can in most cases go ahead without any involvement by the Commission.

Exempt charities have never had to obtain the Commission's consent, but may be required to obtain the consent of some other body, for example the Housing Corporation in the case of a registered housing association.

Consent is not required where the charity disposes of land to another charity, or leases it to a beneficiary, in accordance with the express provisions in the trusts. There is also no need for consent where the transaction is authorised by an Act of Parliament or a scheme made by the Commission (or the court).

In all other cases, consent is always required where the other party to the transaction is one of the trustees; or a donor to the charity; or a person closely connected by a family or business relationship with a trustee or donor; or where the charity will not get the best price or rent obtainable; or where the procedures laid down in the legislation cannot, for some reason, be carried out. In those cases, consent must be obtained *before* the trustees commit themselves to the deal and the Commission, who will need to be satisfied that the transaction is in the charity's interests, will inform the trustees of their detailed requirements.

3.7.2.1 New procedure

In the majority of cases, the trustees will have to follow the required procedures which are designed to safeguard both the charity and the trustees personally. Before committing themselves to any transaction (ie in the case of a sale, before exchanging contracts), the trustees must instruct an independent, qualified surveyor (who may be the estate agent who finds the purchaser for the charity but not the agent who approaches the charity on behalf of a prospective purchaser) to make a written report on the proposed transaction, which covers all the items listed in the regulations including the measurements of the land, any planning permission, and the value of the land, and to advise on the best method of marketing and disposing of the land. The trustees must then carry out any marketing recommended by the surveyor, for example by placing notices at the site or in the local newspaper and reach a positive decision that the proposed terms are the best that the charity can obtain. Only then may the trustees commit themselves to the transaction.

In the case of functional land held on a formal trust for use for charitable purposes, a sale, exchange or long lease should not normally take place unless the trust contains a power of sale (or leasing), since this is inconsistent with a straightforward trust to use the land for a specified purpose. If there is no power of sale, it may be possible to find that it is implied in the particular circumstances, such as where the sale will *not* mean that the charity ceases to hold and use land for a charitable purpose. Otherwise, the Charity Commission may be willing to make a scheme to confer an express power. If there is a power of sale and the purpose of the sale is not simply to buy a replacement property, additional steps must be carried out before the land is sold. Whatever marketing arrangements are made the trustees must advertise the proposed sale and invite comments from the public. They must then consider any objections or suggestions received from the public before proceeding.

Simpler arrangements are permitted for short leases without a premium. A lease for up to seven years may be granted without a written report from a surveyor and the surveyor need not be formally qualified as long as the trustees are satisfied that he or she has the necessary knowledge and experience and the terms are the best that can be obtained for the charity. A lease for up to two years, of land held on trust for functional purposes, need not be specifically advertised.

3.7.2.2 Formalities

Specific formalities must be followed in the actual contract, agreement, lease, conveyance, deed of gift or transfer, whenever land is acquired or disposed of by a charity, including an exempt charity. These are designed to make it clear whether the land is subject to the restrictions imposed by law and, in the case of dispositions, whether the procedures have been followed. This is not, therefore, an area of conveyancing which the lay person can expect to be able to undertake without legal advice.

3.7.3   Mortgage of land

Apart from being an investment or a charitable facility, charity land can be a valuable financial resource in the sense that it can be mortgaged in order to secure a loan (for example to fund a project). The Charities Act 1993 (as amended by Charities Act 2006) lays down a procedure for borrowing on the security of charity land without the need for the Charity Commission's consent. This involves obtaining advice from a financial expert (who must be entirely unconnected with the lender but may be an employee of the charity) concerning the charity's need to borrow, whether the rate of interest is reasonable and whether the charity can afford the loan charges.

3.7.4   Disposal of land (Scotland)

As Scotland does not have a Charity Commission, there are no specific restrictions on sale by charities of their property. However, the disposal of land and general dealings between a charity and a trustee will be restricted by the trust deed or, in the case of a charitable company, its articles of association.

A registered housing association, which is also a charity, will require the consent of the organisation Scottish Homes to the grant or disposal of its land or, indeed, the granting of any security over that land.

The general restrictions applicable to English charities are not applicable to Scottish charities.

3.8   MAKING GRANTS

Some charities operate entirely by giving grants of money or other forms of financial assistance to individuals or to other charities for furtherance of the charitable purposes of those charities. Some of the smallest and some of the largest charities in the UK operate in this way. Others make occasional grants or loans. If charity money is to be used effectively, sensible methods of selecting recipients, fixing the level and period of support, and following up the way in which the grant has been used should be adopted.

3.8.1   Objective of grant

First, consideration must be given to the objective of the assistance proposed. This will depend on the purpose of the awarding charity, which may be very specific, for example relieving need in a particular area, or very general, such as furthering any charitable purpose at the discretion of the trustees. The purpose of the charity sets the limits for grant making but, in most cases, since funds are never unlimited, the trustees must take a policy decision on the kinds of grant they will normally consider. Policy decisions are not fixed, and policy decisions are often modified from time to time in the light of experience, the needs of potential recipients and the resources available.

3.8.2 Applications for assistance

Secondly, the trustees must decide whether they will invite applications or find other ways of identifying recipients. This depends largely on the breadth of the purpose and area of benefit and on how close the charity, or its trustees, are to the proposed beneficiaries. In the case of a local charity, it may be preferable for the trustees or their staff to find individual beneficiaries through local schools, churches or other organisations, or the local authority, rather than to seek applications. This is important particularly where there may be some doubt about whether those most in need of help will come forward by themselves. In a large area, and where grants are normally given to charities rather than individuals, postal applications are usual. In those cases, care is needed in targeting potentially successful applicants and designing the application form (if any) to enable the applications to be considered efficiently.

3.8.3 Policy guidelines

When a charity has numerous applications to consider the policy guidelines assist in reducing the number to manageable proportions and it may be sensible to divide the task of giving detailed consideration and carrying out any further investigations between different members of the trustee body. It is the trustees as a whole, however, who are responsible for the allocation of funds.

It is always wise to check out various issues, such as the other sources of funds available to an applicant; the effect (if any) which the proposed assistance will have, in the case of individuals, on any statutory benefits to which they are entitled; and, in the case of grants to charities, whether they have complied with their obligations to register and submit accounts. It is also prudent to find out exactly what the money will be used for and, in cases of grants to charities, to check that the proposals are within the objects of the recipient charities. These precautions help to ensure that the grant will be effective.

Not every recipient will be well enough organised to manage the grant if it is paid in one lump sum and, in any case, the grant-making charity may not have the whole amount available at once. In such cases, the payments may be made by instalment and the grant-making charity may wish to impose conditions, such as receiving an account or a school report, and checking that the grant is being used effectively before paying out future instalments. It is not uncommon for grants to be paid over three years or longer.

Monitoring the use made of grants, by means of spot checks, questionnaires and follow-up correspondence, is generally worthwhile, since it enables the trustees to keep a check on the effectiveness of the grant and modify their policy and procedures for the future. Provided that the amount is not excessive, the additional time and money will be well spent.

Effectiveness is not everything, however. Unlike statutory bodies spending taxpayers' money under bureaucratic controls, charities are in the fortunate position of being speedy, imaginative and able to conduct small-scale experiments from time to time. They do not exist to ape the provision made by central or local government, but have their own agenda in which they can give help or take initiatives which the statutory system cannot attempt. Independence is a boon, which should be valued. Charities can be originators, experts and leaders in their own fields.

A suggested form of grant agreement between one charity and another appears in Appendix A.

3.9   RAISING FUNDS

Most new charities are not endowed by their founders but must raise funds in order to survive and grow. Some charities need to raise funds for particular projects from time to time. Fortunately, people are often generous when they are convinced that their gifts will be put to good use, or they may merely be attracted by enthusiastic, heart-warming or heart-touching advertisements.

In addition, the National Lottery has provided a means of collecting money for good causes on a vast scale. Charities may apply for grants (usually given on the basis that a similar amount is found from other sources) to the National Lottery Charities Board or (where appropriate) UK Sport, the National Heritage Memorial Fund or the Millennium Commission.

Fundraising is not in itself a charitable purpose, so an organisation set up purely to raise funds is not a charity. However, moderate fundraising, including expenditure for that purpose, is allowable as part of the administration of a charity. If fundraising is likely to involve a substantial amount of cost and effort, and certainly where it will dominate the activities of the charity, it is wise to set up a separate organisation to carry it out (see 'Trading' at **3.12** below).

3.9.1 Managing fundraising

Managing the raising of funds has its own expertise, and trustees should not assume that they can be successful fundraisers without taking advice from someone who knows about the problems involved. On the other hand, trustees should be wary of committing themselves to a commercial fundraiser without checking his or her credentials. So many charities have had disastrous experiences with cynical or incompetent 'professionals' that enhanced controls have been introduced to regulate the sort of agreement which is allowed and require disclosure of fundraisers' remuneration. A charity (or its trustees) cannot be held to an agreement which does not comply with the law. It is hoped that the revised régime will increase public confidence as well as the confidence of the charities themselves.

3.9.2 Methods of fundraising

There are as many ways of raising funds as human ingenuity can devise and, as with so many other activities, there are fashions which change from time to time. Generally, it is easier to raise money for a cause which appeals to the emotions of prospective donors, and for a specific project rather than for basic running costs. Additional incentives may be provided if the beneficiaries and/or donors are involved in some specific activity, which can be entertaining or instructive in itself, or by the provision of prizes or rewards. Occasionally, two or more charities may combine their efforts in a creative way which helps to place their work in a different perspective.

3.9.3 Restrictions on fundraising

The law impinges on particular types of fundraising activities in different ways:

(1) The regular buying and selling of goods or services is considered 'trading' and, unless it is carried out in actually furthering the objects of the charity or by the beneficiaries (see under 'Tax and rates' at 3.4 above) it will be taxable. Small-scale, one-off or occasional trading, such as a jumble sale, a Scouts job week or an annual sale of Christmas cards is acceptable, however.

(2) If a professional fundraiser or commercial organisation solicits funds for a charity by means of a broadcast or over the telephone, it is obligatory to provide an opportunity for someone who contributes £50 or more (in the case of a broadcast only if by credit or debit card) to cancel the payment within seven days, and, where goods have been purchased, when they have been returned.

(3)   Lotteries are illegal unless the charity is registered with the Gaming
       Board or the lottery is conducted within the prescribed limits as a
       small lottery, private lottery or society's lottery.

(4)   Advertising and broadcasting is subject to the law of libel and the
       advertising and broadcasting Codes of Practice, which reflect public
       opinion on what is fair and decent. As with all advertising,
       exaggerated claims tend to be counter-productive.

(5)   It is wise for charities to beware of political controversy; although
       views may be strongly held within the organisation itself, it is not the
       purpose of any charity to campaign for a change in the law, either in
       the UK or elsewhere. In addition, the expression of seemingly
       political views is likely to be off-putting to potential supporters.

(6)   Local and road safety regulations may need to be checked where an
       outdoor activity, such as a bicycle ride, is planned, and permission
       from landowners affected will be required.

(7)   Health and safety regulations, food regulations and licensing laws, as
       well as the detailed terms of hiring and insuring premises will be
       relevant where premises are to be used for a sale, a dance or other
       event which is likely to attract large numbers.

(8)   If funds are to be collected from the public by house-to-house
       collections or in a public place such as the street, a shopping precinct
       or other place to which the public have access without payment, the
       charity will need to obtain a permit from the local authority or the
       police or, if the appeal or flag day is to be nationwide, an order from
       the Home Office. Various conditions are likely to be imposed,
       including, possibly, conditions to protect public order and traffic
       control, and collectors will be required to have badges and
       certificates (sometimes combined in one) to prove that they are
       genuine. The law in this area was overhauled by the Charities
       Act 1992, Part III, but those rules are not in force and will be
       replaced by provisions in the Charities Act 2006.

3.9.4   Fundraising records

It is vitally important to keep careful records of money raised by
fundraising efforts and the cost of raising it, so as to be able to judge
whether a similar effort should be made another time and to report back
quickly to supporters on the immediate result, and also to report later on
the use to which the funds have been put. It is questionable whether
charities are right to suggest to supporters that by giving a stated amount
they will enable the charity to do something specific and individual (such
as feed a starving child for a month) but it is useful and valuable to be able
to point to a particular project or initiative which, through money

contributed by the public, has become a reality, and it is arguable that a greater public response will be encouraged if the donors can share the charity's feeling of achievement.

Several of the larger national charities capitalise on this by setting up or encouraging the formation of local or regional 'branches' or groups of 'friends' whose main practical function is to raise funds for the central organisation. It is usual for these groups to be given permission to quote the national charity's registration number while raising funds. This may be sensible and effective in many cases, but it is worth pointing out that the national body must then take responsibility for whatever is said or done in its name. It should also ensure that it has approved the constitution of the local group (and can control any amendments to it) and that it receives the local group's accounts, which should be incorporated into the national body's own accounts.

3.9.5   Fundraising agreements

3.9.5.1   *England and Wales*

Part II of the Charities Act 1992 and the regulations made under it introduced controls on 'professional fundraisers' and 'commercial participators'. A professional fundraiser is a person or firm which carries on business as a fundraiser or is engaged to raise funds for a fee amounting to at least £500 pa or per project, or at least £5 per day. It does not include an employee of the charity concerned.

A commercial participator is any person or organisation (except a professional fundraiser) which carries on any kind of business, and uses a charity connection in an advertising or sales campaign, or other promotional venture, for example a business which advertises that part of the price of its goods will be given to charity. This does not include a charity's trading subsidiary.

The legislation is enacted to protect the public by ensuring that when they are asked to give to a charity, or support a charity, by a professional fundraiser or commercial participator, they will know how much of what they contribute will go to the charity, and how much to the professional or commercial organisation. When soliciting funds or promoting goods or services, the professional fundraiser or commercial participator is obliged by law to state the basis of his remuneration or the percentage of profit that will actually reach the charity which is intended to benefit, and must specify what charity or charities will benefit. In addition, agreements with charities by professional fundraisers and commercial participators must contain certain specific provisions, or they will not be enforceable against the charity.

Before entering into a fundraising agreement, therefore, it is wise for a charity to seek professional advice from someone other than the fundraiser concerned.

3.9.5.2   *Scotland*

There are no equivalent regulations in Scotland, although a voluntary Scottish Code of Practice was published in 1995 by the Scottish Council for Voluntary Organisations and the Institute of Fundraising. The Code extends the requirement for written agreements beyond 'professional fundraisers' and 'commercial partners' to include external advisers and consultants. Accountants and lawyers should take heed.

3.9.6   Offences

Under Part III of the Charities Act 1992 it is an offence to collect funds from the public without a local authority permit or a Charity Commission order or to fail to comply with the regulations about public collections for charity. It is also an offence to solicit funds for an organisation which is stated to be a registered charity when it is not. Furthermore, a charity which discovers that an unauthorised person is collecting funds on its behalf is able to apply to the court for an order to prevent it.

The 1992 Act does not apply to Scotland, but again, the voluntary Code of Practice achieves a similar effect.

3.10   ACCEPTING GIFTS AND LEGACIES

It might be supposed that there are no problems for a charity in accepting gifts and legacies. However, it is sometimes necessary to give the matter careful thought.

There may be technical problems connected with gifts and legacies. A gift of anything other than money must be made in the correct manner and in favour of the correct person. There can be serious difficulties in the case of gifts by will if the recipient charity is incorrectly described, and in such cases there may even be competition between charities for the gift.

Sometimes, it is not clear whether a specific charity is referred to in a will. In Scotland, the matter may have to go to court. In England and Wales, the procedure depends on whether or not the gift takes the form of a trust (including a trust to administer the residue of an estate). If there is a trust, the Charity Commission will deal with the matter and a scheme may be required. They should be approached direct.

If there is a simple gift (for example to 'cancer research') without any trust, the executors should apply in the first instance to the Treasury Solicitor (Charities Division). The Treasury Solicitor acts for the Attorney-General, who can then use a procedure under the Royal Sign Manual (which he operates for the Queen) to direct the gift to a suitable charity or purpose.

In most cases, there will be some indication of the charity, or the sort of charity, which the testator wished to benefit. It is helpful to the Commission or the Treasury Solicitor to know which charity or charities the testator supported during his or her lifetime.

It is rare for such problems to be referred to the court and, of course, it is desirable that they should not be in view of the costs inevitably incurred, which reduce the amount available for charity.

3.10.1 Refusal to accept gifts

Occasionally, the trustees of a charity, for some good reason, decide that they do not wish the charity to accept a gift. The trustees are not entitled to refuse a gift unless it is impractical or would entail a liability which would outweigh its value. In England and Wales, if there is some other reason not to accept it, the trustees should seek the advice of the Charity Commission, which may authorise them to decline it. The risk for the trustees if they do not obtain that authority is that, at some later date, they might be required to make good to the charity the amount which their action had caused it to forgo.

3.10.2 Gifts subject to conditions

If the gift is subject to a condition or expressed to be for some particular purpose which does not enable the trustees to pool it with the rest of the charity's resources it may be necessary to register the gift as a 'subsidiary charity' (ie one which is technically a separate charity and which is administered alongside an existing registered charity), and show it separately in the accounts. This happens frequently in the case of school charities, to which former staff and pupils often give a prize fund for particular subjects or sports.

The same principle applies in the case of funds given for a specific purpose during the lifetime of the donor or funds raised by an appeal for a specific project. The money or property which has been given to the charity is held by the trustees on a special trust for that purpose and cannot be treated as part of the charity's general funds.

3.10.2.1   *Failure of purpose*

When the funds available cannot reasonably be used for the specified purpose, for example where the cost is too great or planning permission is refused, it is not open to the trustees simply to use the funds for other purposes, unless the terms of the gift or the appeal literature specifically allow for this. In strict law, in these situations the trustees hold the funds on behalf of the donors. If there is a single, identifiable, living donor the problem may quite easily be resolved by going back to him or her, explaining the problem and requesting permission (preferably in writing) to use the funds for another purpose of the charity.

If, on the other hand, it is not possible to identify or trace all the donors, for example where the money has come from cash collections or from a fundraising concert or other event or where the donor is no longer alive, the purpose can only be altered by a scheme.

There are two procedures associated with the making of a scheme in this situation, outlined below, depending on whether the gift is made by will or otherwise.

3.10.2.2   *'General charitable intention'*

If the gift is made by will the normal procedure, which avoids an application to the court, is first to determine whether there was a 'general charitable intention' on the part of the testator. If so, it is best to reach an agreement between the charity and the residuary beneficiaries or persons who would be entitled on intestacy, then to obtain the approval of the Treasury Solicitor acting for the Attorney-General on a destination for the fund which is cy-près the testator's intention, and then to ask the Charity Commission to make a scheme to direct the funds for that purpose. The executors will be in charge of the funds and will normally carry out the correspondence until the scheme is made.

3.10.2.3   *Identifiable donors*

If the funds have been raised by an appeal, a scheme will not be made until all identifiable donors are contracted and asked either to sign a written disclaimer or ask for their money back. When the scheme has been established the trustees will have to put any funds given by donors who could not be contacted aside for six months. This procedure has been streamlined by regulations under the Charities Act 1992, and details of the regulations are available from the Charity Commission.

3.10.3 Avoiding failure

In view of the potential difficulties, which can be time-consuming and expensive for the charity, it is prudent to offer advice and guidance to would-be donors, informing them of the purposes for which gifts would be welcome and, above all, making the proper name and address of the charity quite clear to them. It may also help to identify a charity by its registered number in addition to its name. Most problems arise where a charity changes its name (or address) or where its publicity material is vague or inaccurate on technical details. In the case of appeals, it is sensible to state an alternative purpose in case the appeal fails to reach or overshoots its target or if the project in question cannot be carried out at the end of the day, and to ask donors to state, when making their contributions, whether they wish to have their money returned in such an event.

3.11 PATRONS AND SPONSORS

Artists, composers and architects have all relied on the patronage, ie material support and protection, of wealthy and well-placed individuals. From the Enlightenment onwards, charities of all kinds have often had patrons. Today, the patronage of a member of the Royal Family, a media star or a representative of excellence in the charity's field of work is regarded by many charities as a valuable asset which can ensure that the charity is taken seriously, adds dignity to formal occasions and helps in fundraising.

The role of the patron, however, does not now involve the direct provision of cash or commissions. This function has been taken over by the sponsor.

A sponsor is more likely to be a commercial organisation than an individual and is more often limited to a specific project, such as the publication of the charity's newsletter, the provision of equipment to be used by the charity or the support of a particular fundraising event, and is also limited in terms of the amount of support provided. In addition, the sponsor expects to receive a tangible benefit for itself, such as increased public awareness of its goods or services, from its association with the charity.

All kinds of odd combinations, some witty, result from sponsorship agreements by charities, which can be very beneficial to both parties. Care is needed, however, in the initial choice of sponsor, since its own reputation will be linked with the charity's and it could, for example, be embarrassing if an environmental charity was sponsored by an industrial concern which turned out to be a polluter, or a temperance charity was sponsored by a multi-purpose company which diversified into alcoholic drinks. Charities should also be wary of being so grateful for the sponsorship that they allow the sponsor's name to dominate the charity's publicity. If charitable funds are used to any substantial extent to promote a non-charitable body, the trustees could be liable for a breach of trust and the charity could be taxed on the amount spent.

3.11.1 'Commercial participators'

The Charities Act 1992, Part II, contains requirements for 'commercial participators' which, like professional fundraisers, are obliged to disclose how much of any promotion, which is stated to be for charity, will actually be given to charity. Commercial supporters caught by these provisions are not able to get away with the suggestion that all or most of the proceeds of something they sell will be used for charity unless this is strictly true.

3.12 TRADING

Some charities pursue trading activities in their charitable work. For instance, a charity which runs workshops for disabled people as a method of relieving their disability is carrying out a trade if the goods produced are sold. Similarly, a charity for educational purposes may operate through a fee-paying school or other institution, and it is also common to find the league of friends of a hospital providing extra comforts for the patients by means of a hospital shop or flower stall. However, there are unlikely to be any tax or legal difficulties in these cases.

3.12.1 Trading activities as adjunnct to charitable purpose

Where, for example, a university contracts to carry out research for a commercial organisation, a cathedral sells art books or souvenirs or a bar is established in a community centre, the trading activity may enhance, as well as help to finance, the charitable purpose but is an adjunct to, rather than a method of carrying out, the charitable purpose. Caution must be exercised if a trading activity of this kind becomes successful or begins to assume importance as an element in the charity's finances. If the trend continues, it will be necessary to consider hiving off the trading activity to a separate, non-charitable body – usually, but not necessarily, a limited company.

3.12.2 Trading for the purpose of raising funds

Trading which is carried out purely for the purpose of raising funds need have nothing to do with the work or purpose of the charity, although it will often promote its name. For example, the sale of T-shirts and other promotional goods, the issue of gift catalogues, a dining club, a second-hand clothes shop or even a specific business, such as publishing or estate agency, may be conducted exclusively in support of a charity.

This does not make the trade a charitable purpose, nor can an organisation devoted to that trade be a charity, even if all the profits are used for wholly charitable purposes. The trading company will not, however, be a 'commercial participator' for the purposes of the Charities Act 1992, if it is controlled by the charity, for example if the charity owns the majority of the shares (see **3.12** above).

It follows that a charity is not in a position to use its funds to support the trading activity since this would normally be an application of funds for a non-charitable purpose and a breach of trust. There are rare exceptions. The purchase of shares in a trading company or the making of a loan at a market rate of interest to a trading body can, in some circumstances, be regarded as a proper investment for the funds of the charity, assuming that its powers of investment are wide enough to permit this and satisfactory financial advice is obtained. In most cases, however, the fact that the charity is asked to provide financial support is an indication of economic weakness on the trading company's part and should sound a clear warning to the trustees that the charity should not allow itself to become too dependent on the trading company or too closely connected with its problems. It is better for the trading body to obtain its finance from an independent source.

When the arrangements are working satisfactorily, they can prove very beneficial. The preferred system is for the trading body, which may be a company or, for example, a social club, to covenant the whole or part of its taxable profits to the charity for a period of at least three years. As a result, the trading body is relieved from tax on the amount paid each year and the charity is entitled to recover the amount in question from HMRC.

In addition, the charitable relief from non-domestic rates is available for charity shops and commercial outlets within charity premises, and VAT reliefs may be available.

CHAPTER 4

MANAGEMENT

4.1 CHOOSING TRUSTEES

Although the trustees themselves may not consider the personality of trustees to be important (and charity employees may have a sneaking preference for the kind of trustee who remains in the background), the character of the governing body of a charity is a key to the character and reputation of the charity and may be vital to its success or failure.

People become trustees for a variety of reasons, often subjective, and in a variety of ways, often serendipitous. In some cases they are elected by the members or appointed by outside bodies, such as the local authority, or from the beneficiary class, such as patients suffering from a specific disease or their families or the users of facilities provided by the charity for the community. In such cases, there may be an opportunity for the continuing trustees to influence the appointment or even suggest a particular person. In other cases, the trustees are appointed by the continuing trustees directly.

Generally, it is helpful if the trustees have something in common with each other, since this eases communication between them and tends to minimise the scope for sterile arguments about peripheral issues. The most important common interest should, of course, be a sincere desire to carry out the charity's purposes effectively, but successful teamwork can be built up if the trustees also have a specific geographical or religious link, even where the charity is not confined to a particular locality or a particular religious denomination.

There are dangers for the well-being of the charity, however, if the trustees are too closely identified with each other, and especially if two or more of them are related (unless, of course, the charity is a family charity). There are also serious risks of stagnation if the same people remain in office as trustees for years on end, especially where they are all of a similar age.

Ideally, a body of trustees should not be a monoculture but should contain representatives of different occupations, age groups, sexes and social backgrounds, with a regular turnover so that no one becomes indispensable and thus trapped, and new ideas are constantly being brought into the discussions. Arrangements vary, but three years is a reasonable term of office and it is wise to adopt a system under which trustees are required to have a break from their duties after two consecutive terms of office. It should also be possible for trustees to resign when their own circumstances change, without feeling that they are placing an unfair burden on their co-trustees.

The risk of taking on an unknown colleague can be avoided if, in advance of any formal appointment, a prospective trustee is invited to attend a few meetings as an observer. A similar compromise may provide a sympathetic solution to the problem of an elderly trustee, who can no longer be expected to take an active part in the administration of the charity but for whom complete retirement would cause a serious sense of loss.

The qualities which a charity trustee should ideally possess are: genuine concern, rather than cynicism; reliability and judgement, since other people will be affected by the trustees' decisions; a willingness to listen and learn, since in the charity world new developments are taking place constantly; and a measure of toughness in order to safeguard the charity's interests. To the extent that such paragons are not always available, these qualities can be provided in combination by the whole trustee body.

It will also be appropriate to look for specific qualities required by the purposes, organisation and needs of the particular charity. Thus, it is useful to have a medical practitioner on the body of trustees of a charity which promotes medical research or care for the sick, a landowner or property expert where the charity's assets include land and buildings; a mother or teacher where the charity is concerned with young children; and so forth. Any charity can benefit from the contribution of a sympathetic accountant, lawyer or company secretary. Apart from the direct contribution to the trustees' own decision-making, a trustee's expertise can also be useful to the work of any member of the staff of the charity who has the same or a relevant profession or function.

4.2   TRUSTEE MEETINGS

The essence of the decision-making process within a charity is the meeting of the trustees. The conduct of meetings may be laid down in detail in the governing instrument, in which case the requirements should be strictly followed but, in addition, charities tend to develop their own traditions, which differ widely. In all cases, the essentials of an effective meeting are adequate preparation, fair and efficient chairmanship and accurate, readable minutes. This applies whether the meeting is held in person or (as the constitution may permit) by means of a telephone conference or other electronic media.

4.2.1 Preparation

Before the meeting, the clerk or secretary, or the director of the charity (who in many cases performs the secretarial function at trustee meetings) should discuss with the chairman the proposed agenda, the order in which items should appear and the timing of the meeting. It is as well to have a proposed time for the end of the meeting as well as the beginning. The notice of the date and time of the meeting, the agenda and any supporting papers should normally be sent to each of the trustees in ample time for them to arrange their diaries and study the papers.

Trustees should be encouraged to give their apologies in advance if they are unable to attend, since this may affect the quorum. In some cases, a meeting may need to be arranged to suit the timetable of a particular trustee who has some special contribution to make to an item on the agenda.

There is no reason why those who cannot attend should not be invited to give their views in advance, but it must always be remembered that they will not have heard the discussion and cannot veto a decision by that means.

Meetings should be held in a quiet environment, with adequate space and where the trustees will not be interrupted.

4.2.2 Quorum

There must be a quorum if the meeting is to take any decisions. Where a meeting is unexpectedly inquorate, it is often worthwhile to continue with the discussion, with a view to ratification of any provisional decisions at the next meeting.

Some trustee bodies do not find it necessary to put a matter to the vote, whilst other bodies vote on every point; it is a matter of style and tradition. Voting should normally be by a show of hands or other tangible indication of preference, given only after full discussion has taken place.

4.2.3 Chairmanship

The chairman's rôle is to conduct the meeting and see that it gets through its business. The purpose of the casting vote is not to give the chairman extra powers but to enable him or her to end the discussion on a particular item. For this reason, the convention is that the chairman should not use the casting vote to alter an existing policy or to impose a controversial decision on the trustees. This does not mean that the chairman should be passive. In many case, the chairman exercises leadership which is appreciated by his or her fellow trustees and helps the charity to operate in a dynamic way. On the other hand, the chairman must be fair and try to encourage all the trustees (even recently appointed trustees) to participate.

There will be occasions when it is desirable to invite a person other than the trustees and their secretary to attend a meeting. For example, the meeting may provide a suitable occasion to hear, at first hand, the advice of a professional adviser, or a particular employee may have a report to make or explain. Whatever the trustees' normal habits at meetings, it is worth bearing in mind that the person who has been invited is the trustees' guest for the occasion and should be shown courtesy; he or she should not, for example, be kept waiting and should not be expected to sit through irrelevant agenda items.

4.2.4 Minutes

Minutes should always be taken, since they will constitute the record of what was decided and may have to be referred to at a later date. They may be taken by the secretary, clerk or director or by a trustee or employee chosen for the purpose. They should not be taken by the chairman.

The arrangements should ensure that, within reason, the trustees feel free to speak their minds at the meeting. It is important that the minutes record only what is likely to be useful for the charity's records. Therefore, it is preferable that the minutes are taken by a person, rather than a mindless tape-recorder, transcription from which would, in any case, be an unpleasant chore.

It is normal practice for the minutes to be circulated in draft to all those who attended the meeting and either approved or corrected at the next meeting, when they should be signed by the chairman. The minutes should then be kept in a safe place and must be available for any trustee to consult.

4.2.5 Frequency of trustee meetings

There should always be at least two meetings of the trustees each year and, in many cases, it will be necessary or desirable to hold considerably more.

The precise arrangements will depend on the nature of the charity's work and the extent to which it is carried out by employees, rather than directly by the trustees. There should, in any case, be a procedure for calling a special meeting at short notice to deal with emergencies. There is no excuse for not dealing with a serious problem merely because the next scheduled meeting of the trustees is some months ahead.

In addition, there may be meetings of committees (who must report to the next full meeting if not before) and the occasional social gathering will help to keep trustees (and others) in touch.

4.3 DEALING WITH PROFESSIONALS

There are numerous occasions in the running of a charity when professional advice is desirable or essential. A charity's needs are different from those of an individual, and trustees, because they are not dealing with their own assets, are more often in the position of requiring professional advice. Obtaining and acting on professional advice can also safeguard the trustees personally from any claim that they have failed in their duties. Trustees should be able to recognise when professional advice should be obtained for the charity and be able, in practice, to obtain it.

4.3.1 Choosing a professional

The correct choice of a professional adviser is vitally important and not always easy. The quality and style of professional people varies considerably and the best recommendation is always one from a similar organisation based on personal experience. In addition to being satisfied of the competence of the adviser and, where appropriate, of professional qualifications and other credentials, trustees must consider two particular factors: fees, and the chemistry of the relationship.

4.3.1.1 Fees

Professional services cost money and it is a false economy to assume that being a charity is a passport to free advice of adequate quality. A trustee would not expect to employ, for example, a builder, to work for nothing. Fees are almost always likely to be higher than the trustees think, but they are a proper administrative expense which can and should be budgeted for. It is, therefore, essential to accept that there will be a financial cost and to make sure, at the outset, that the amount involved is known (in broad terms) and that the charity can afford that cost. Nor should trustees suppose that just because their meetings are not frequent the professional will be happy to wait for payment until the next meeting is held.

4.3.1.2 Relationship between adviser and trustees

It is essential that the individual who advises the trustees commands their respect and trust. All professional relationships require confidence on both sides and in order to be effective the trustees and senior staff must be able to work with their adviser, discuss the charity's affairs frankly and openly with him or her and take seriously the advice provided.

4.3.2   Effectiveness

Having chosen a professional adviser, it is in the charity's interests that the most effective use should be made of his or her services, both to obtain the best advice for the charity and to avoid wasted costs. For day-to-day contact it is most efficient if there is a single representative of the charity who normally deals directly with the adviser. There will be occasions when a meeting with a group of the trustees (or even with the whole trustee body) is desirable, but this is more useful for general information gathering and background than for more specific points.

A professional should not be presumed to have any more knowledge of the charity and its problems or priorities than the trustees provide. It may, therefore, be sensible to start the relationship with a written summary of the background and, in many cases, a copy of the charity's governing instrument(s) and latest report and statement of accounts. A meeting at an early stage will be helpful to clarify any points which remain in doubt and to consider the precise problem in more detail. There is no reason to assume that an initial consultation should be free of charge. Very often, the first meeting with an experienced professional will direct the charity towards the solution.

Communications thereafter will remain of prime importance. The professional will need information from time to time and this should be readily available. Letters and telephone messages should be answered promptly. The professional should also be notified of any relevant changes in the situation and kept informed generally of the charity's progress.

A good working relationship with the charity's professional advisers can be an enormous asset to the charity, but like any other relationship it needs to be nurtured and developed.

4.3.3   Problems with advisers

If there are any problems in the trustees' relationship with the adviser, he or she, or the senior partner in the adviser's firm, should be told at once and action taken to resolve the problems. There is often a simple remedy and there is, of course, no excuse for complaining of poor service only when the invoice arrives.

If, as sometimes happens for a variety of reasons, the trustees reach the conclusion that they will not stay with a particular professional adviser, they should take action to terminate the relationship at once rather than allow the relationship to deteriorate. They should remember, however, that it is unlikely that their papers will be returned until they have paid any outstanding fees.

If the worst comes to the worst, the trustees may have to consider taking legal action against a professional for loss caused to the charity through negligence. They will require prompt advice from an independent solicitor on any such move.

4.3.4 Mistakes to avoid

It is up to the trustees to consult a professional as soon as a problem or potential problem appears. It is not wise to leave the consultation until the trustees have tried, and failed, to solve it themselves, thereby making the situation more complex and difficult to solve. Neither must the trustees simply ignore the problem, hoping that it will go away. Even if a particular difficulty does not materialise, it will be useful to have obtained advice for a future occasion, and the trustees may learn something beneficial to the charity in the course of obtaining the advice.

Trustees should avoid the error of thinking that they know the answer before they have asked the question. Sometimes they will find that they have asked the wrong question and that the answer is not what they had expected. In order to make the most of advice received they should keep an open mind and be prepared to listen as well as to speak.

There are few outcomes more frustrating for a professional person than to give careful, reasoned advice only for it to be ignored for some subjective reason. The occasions on which professional advice should not be followed are rare: such an outcome will usually be a waste of time for all concerned as well as a waste of the charity's money. If the reasons for the advice are not understood, the trustees should request a further, written, explanation.

On the other hand, trustees should not go to the extreme of passing on to a professional adviser the responsibility for deciding an issue of policy which is properly within their discretion. A professional will be an expert in his or her field, but the trustees remain the experts in their charity, and the decision-makers for it.

4.3.5 Particular specialists

Particular types of profession or business have their own requirements and charities should be aware that there may be special considerations or limitations.

Banking, for example, has been going through a period of rapid change with increased use of new technology. It is prudent to discuss how the charity can make the most effective use of the available services, as well as keeping costs to a minimum, and trustees should be willing to consider modifications to the charity's practices (for example by paying in all donations at a single point) to achieve these ends.

Solicitors vary enormously from the general 'High Street' practitioners to the highly specialised City firm. An increasing number are becoming familiar with charity matters but it is wise to ask.

Barristers may only be instructed via another professional person, ie a solicitor or (in an increasing number of cases) by direct professional access through an accountant, surveyor or chartered secretary or other professional authorised to give instructions.

There is a proliferation of para-legal services which may appear more attractive on cost grounds than consulting a solicitor. However, it is worth bearing in mind that charity law is a specialist area which the average licensed conveyancer, for example, may not readily be able to research. Similarly, a design consultant does not have the same training as an architect.

Charity consultants, including fundraising consultants, of whom there are a great number, do not necessarily have any professional qualification or supervision. The National Council for Voluntary Organisations ('NCVO') maintains a list of consultants covering a variety of fields, and the Institute of Fundraising has a register of members and is also publishing a handbook. Particular care is required when choosing an appropriate consultant and entering into an agreement. It may be sensible to contact other charities who have used consultants on similar projects, and to obtain advice on the form of agreement, or at least check for hidden 'extras'. It is usually unwise to commit the charity to a long-term contract. It should also be remembered that consultants should not normally be paid a retainer as opposed to an hourly or daily rate.

Investment advisers must be informed of the charity's investment powers and of the investment policy which the trustees propose to follow. Trustees should not assume that the charity will obtain a better deal by agreeing to pay commission rather than fees and should also be wary of hidden 'extra' charges.

4.3.6   Beauty parades

The expression 'beauty parade' is commonly used in the commercial world to describe a method of choosing between competing professionals by asking them to present what they offer. All professionals are in competition to an extent, but it will not be sensible to use this method of choosing between them unless the charity is able to provide a very clear brief of what it requires. It should also be recognised that, unless the charity is looking for the qualities of a good salesman, a beauty parade may not disclose the relevant strengths and weaknesses of the competitors. Other methods are simply to inquire carefully and to compare several estimates.

4.4 EMPLOYEES AND VOLUNTEERS

For all but the smallest charities, the manpower provided by the trustees alone is not enough. Workers, paid or unpaid, must be recruited. In fact, many of the most prominent and influential people in the charity world today are employees rather than trustees.

Unfortunately, charities in general do not have a good track record in this sphere – there is a relatively fast turnover among charity employees. One of the reasons for this is simple lack of thought; it need not be so.

In order to attract good people to work for a charity, the charity needs to demonstrate that it can provide a satisfactory working environment, something it cannot easily do until it has discovered its own management style.

As usual, the responsibility falls on the trustees. They set the pace, indicate the expectations, decide on the rewards and, as the charity grows, choose the leaders who, in due course, will be doing much of this on their own initiative, and building up the charity's corporate culture and traditions.

It is worth using a little imagination on this topic. From the charity's point of view, the work must be done as effectively and efficiently as possible. No one should suppose that working for a charity is an easy option or that competition or its equivalent does not apply. If, however, the workers are looked upon as mere human resources, it is easy to make the mistake of demoralising them by over-work or unrealistic targets, which is likely to result in the opposite of the intended outcome.

4.4.1 Interviewing candidates

Interviewing candidates for positions is a skill which can be learned or which can be bought in especially for the occasion. Some charities have found the specialist recruitment consultancies helpful (see Appendix C), but it is as well if the trustees have given thought to the sorts of qualities, qualifications or skills which they are looking for to carry out the job in hand. In formal terms this is called a 'person specification'.

What, then, do workers need in order to give their best for the optimum length of time? In many cases, working for a charity brings its own reward, in the sense that the job is in itself worthwhile. That indicates a need to involve workers in the charity's goals and achievements.

4.4.2 Freedom from insecurity

Freedom from insecurity is provided, in the case of employees, by their contract of employment, which is required by law, and, in the case of both employees and volunteers, by coherent and predictable management arrangements. This can be achieved through consultation, discussion, the employee knowing the extent of his or her responsibilities, a sense of belonging and no sudden surprises.

4.4.3   Freedom from annoyance

In this category can be included all the nagging distractions, from bullying and undue bureaucracy to machinery which does not work. A procedure for airing grievances and a method for improving procedures is essential.

4.4.4   Encouragement or praise when deserved

Employees need to be reassured that their efforts are appreciated. Equally, employees need to be told if their work is not up to standard.

4.4.5   Support for weaknesses

Not everyone is good at everything, and people do not always neatly fit the job. A constructive approach enables the jobs to be modified to fit the people. The experience of volunteering shows that this can work with unpaid jobs too.

4.4.6   Training

The possibility of training or of gaining experience to allow for career development, for example specialist courses, secondments, temporary promotions and special assignments, may all be considered, but simply allowing a junior member of staff or volunteer to exercise some initiative can prove unexpectedly fruitful. (See further **4.8–4.8.6**.)

4.4.7   Fairness

Life may be unfair, but a charity should not be demonstrating that. It is not, in fact, a simple matter to achieve fairness. Goodwill is essential, but there must also be proper job descriptions, systems for appraising jobs and staff, annual reports with built-in checks and balances, an allowance for the differences between people (so that, for example, the loudest voice does not determine priorities) and compliance with race relations and sex discrimination legislation. Charities, generally, do not have such a bad image as some other employers when it comes to ageism.

4.4.8   Remuneration (including pension rights)

Remuneration for employees, should be at, or as near, the going rate for the job as the charity can decently afford. Working for a charity does not remove the material concerns which affect other mortals or diminish family or other responsibilities. Providing housing for employees can be extremely helpful, but it must be borne in mind that the employee will retire in due course and may then wish to have his or her own home.

4.4.9   Health and safety legislation

Health and safety legislation should, of course, be observed, whether the staff are paid or unpaid.

4.4.10   Relationship between director and trustees

The director or chief executive of a substantial charity is in a special position since his or her responsibilities towards the charity mirror those of the trustees themselves, whilst the position affords actual power and control which may exceed that of the trustees. The relationship between the trustees and the director is vitally important. Confidence on both sides is of the first importance, but the director should never be placed in the position of feeling the full weight of responsibility for the charity. He or she must be able to seek guidance, if necessary as a matter of urgency, from the trustees and must be able to look to the trustees to make decisions, particularly decisions on policy. The best ideas and suggestions do not necessarily spring from those who will have to implement them.

4.5   GOOD MANAGEMENT

From the management point of view, charities are not very different from other businesses. It is true that charities do not make money for its own sake, but there will always be some way of measuring their success or lack of it, and their activities have very specific financial implications.

It is wise, as a charity approaches medium size, to take positive steps to plan its management by looking at its resources, actual and potential, its immediate aims and longer-term plans (and the means which are available or which will need to be developed or acquired to achieve them), its philosophy, values and style and how it presents itself.

Planning is by no means enough. Regular reviews and assessments are required and proposals must be placed in an order of priority – and followed up. From time to time, a 'SWOT' analysis is helpful, identifying strengths, weaknesses, opportunities and threats, in order to decide how best to use or cope with them. Sometimes it may be worth examining a perceived weakness to see whether it has any hidden advantages and vice versa. Another strategy is to take a particular activity within the charity, for example information systems, and undertake a thorough review.

4.5.1   Time

Time is generally in short supply: if it is not (and sometimes, of course, if it is) the charity may not be making the best use of it. An annual timetable, or workplan, setting out priorities with published target dates, can help in giving the organisation a sense of direction and coherence, and encourage commitment. Its uses are many, for besides helping the charity to avoid last-minute rushes to meet deadlines for such matters as producing the accounts, it can provide a basis for forward planning, obtaining funds, measuring performance and reorganising working practices. A single policy decision on the time in which letters or applications are answered or whether the unsuccessful applications are to be answered at all, will help to create norms of working and reasonable expectations on the part of applicants and correspondents.

Special care is needed when the charity has outlying groups or branches, or where some of the activities, for example trading or campaigning, have been hived off to separate bodies, which may not themselves be charities.

4.5.2   Contract culture

Additional monitoring systems may well be required where the branches of a national body are involved in the 'contract culture', ie competing with institutions in the private sector in tendering for tasks which would previously have been carried out by local authorities, health authorities or other public bodies. Charities sometimes forget that they do not have a monopoly of care and concern and that private, for-profit organisations may deliver equally good services in the social field. A charity may, indeed, have to resolve difficult problems where its own objects and traditions conflict with the demands of the other contracting party. There is also an observable tendency among public bodies, acting under financial pressure, to try to obtain services at less than a proper fee: the tax relief available to charities may tempt them to accept.

4.5.3   Coherence

Coherence, in the sense that the organisation should have an inner logic, is necessary to avoid confusion about what people are supposed to be doing. Communication, reporting back and accountability within the whole set-up are essential to avoid misunderstanding. Whilst there may be good reasons for the same people to be involved in different aspects of activities, care is needed to ensure that the structures are not allowed to become obscure, or unduly complex. The British Legion, for example, which was the subject of a Charity Commission investigation, was criticised for having an over-complicated committee structure in which some people, wearing different hats, were monitoring themselves, and charitable funds were inadvertently being used to support a non-charitable organisation.

4.5.4   Charity consultants

If trustees find that they have inherited a management structure which seems obscure or difficult, or have any reason to be dissatisfied with the arrangement and cannot readily find a solution, it may be worthwhile to engage the services of a charity consultant or management consultant to investigate, advise and, perhaps, put into place a new system (see 'Particular specialists' at **4.3.5**).

Management should not be seen as an end in itself, but always as a means to furthering the charity's purposes in the most effective way. Nor is it something which is 'done' by one group of people to another. It should involve everyone, including the trustees.

4.6   STATIONERY AND EQUIPMENT

It may be thought that stationery is unimportant and that the content of what is communicated is the charity's only concern. This is not the attitude of the law.

Every registered charity (with an annual gross income of £10,000 or more) is obliged to state the fact that it is a registered charity on all its official documents, including cheques, invoices, receipts and written or printed appeals for funds. It is a punishable offence for a trustee or employee of a charity to authorise the issue of a document which does not comply with this requirement (unless there is a reasonable excuse).

Every limited liability company, charitable or not, is obliged, by company law, to give its full name on all its outgoing documents and, in the case of a charitable company, must state the fact that it is a charity. Non-compliance is an offence.

A charity or a non-charitable body which is registered for VAT should quote its VAT registration number on all invoices and receipts.

These legal requirements can be observed in any reasonable way which the trustees decide, as long as relevant statements are legible and given in English. There is, thus, scope for incorporating them in the design of the stationery and using it to announce or present the charity in a suitable way.

Stationery, which many people will receive, provides the first direct impression about the charity and its style and values. It will be useful to consider particular points, such as whether the paper should be recycled (reflecting concern with environmental issues), whether there should be a logo or script which will give some idea of the charity's purpose or philosophy in encapsulated form, and how much information, for example about patrons, staff or trustees, should be provided on the notepaper (bearing in mind that such details can change).

If the charity provides a service which is of financial value, or even if it merely wishes its work to be identifiable, it is worth considering registration of the design or logo as a service mark at the Trade Marks Registry. A solicitor, patent agent or trade mark agent can be engaged to advise on and make the application, but it is also possible to apply direct, and official guidance is provided.

4.6.1   Cost

The cost of stationery is a major constraint and, again, can be used positively to indicate the charity's concern for economy. It is, in any case, an inexcusable extravagance to use expensive, printed or high quality stationery for internal paperwork.

The paperwork used for seeking funds needs special attention, and may differ according to the person or body to whom it is addressed. Commercially popular, 'glossy' brochures will not necessarily convey the message that the charity needs (as opposed to spends) money. Unduly long and detailed submissions or those which are very closely typed, are not likely to be read in full. A naïvely organised piece of writing will risk conveying the message that funds will also be organised naïvely.

4.6.2   Computers

These days, no mention of stationery is complete without reference to the ubiquitous computer. Computer technology is capable of transforming a charity's efficiency, by cutting out labour-intensive routines. It aids presentation immeasurably, and enables management information of high quality to be provided promptly to decision-makers, thus adding to the charity's professionalism. Just as easily, however, it can lead to obstacles, frustrations and consequential expense. No one is immune from making mistakes, particularly in a rapidly developing field. It is well worth seeking advice, not only from suppliers but also from other organisations performing comparable tasks, before acquiring the equipment or software, and arranging for appropriate training. The Charity Forum (see Appendix C) runs a well-respected charity computer-users group.

Increasingly, charities are using modern forms of communication such as e-mail and the internet. Information provided by such methods may appear authoritative, but it is not subject to independent checks and should be treated with caution. In addition, copyright in material put out over the internet is difficult to protect in view of the ease with which it can be downloaded.

4.7 PREMISES

A charity which is a limited company or friendly or industrial and provident society must have a registered office, clearly marked as such. However, there is no requirement for a charity to have its own actual office or premises and, in fact, many small charities, and some larger, grant-making charities, are administered from the homes of the trustees or the director or from the place of work of a part-time clerk or secretary.

Charities whose work involves the use of land or buildings, or who employ a number of employees (or volunteers) all working together, however, need their own premises. These may be owned or leased or rented or, in some cases, held on a contractual licence which does not amount to a tenancy. They may be used exclusively by the charity or shared with other organisations, including, sometimes, other charities.

4.7.1 Appearance of premises

Where the premises are used for the functional purposes of the charity, for example as a college or hospital or church or veterinary clinic, the functional use will determine the way the accommodation is arranged and will influence the appearance of the building. There can be no better (and no worse) advertisement for the charity than the outside of its functional property (and the interior too, if it is open to the public). It may become a landmark in the district, and it is to be hoped that it will not be an eye-sore. It should also be considered whether the site and building are suitable for the practical requirements of the charity.

Where the premises are the charity's headquarters or office, rather than being directly used to deliver a service to beneficiaries in person, their external appearance and internal functioning are equally important. Like stationery, they give a message to the world at large about the charity's values and approach to its work. In this case, however, the message tends to be a continuing and often permanent one which would be difficult or expensive to alter drastically.

The right sort of message will be conveyed if the approach to the premises is clearly signposted, the entrance accessible (to the disabled as well as the able-bodied) and is neither scruffy nor too imposing. If there are reception arrangements these should put visitors at their ease and, perhaps, include posters, leaflets or other materials which illustrate the charity's work and priorities.

4.7.2 Regulations

Trustees and officers should take care to ensure that they are aware of and comply with all the various regulations regarding the use of office and other buildings and any proposed alterations to them, for example fire regulations, health and safety regulations, building regulations and planning permissions.

Problems foreseen are often avoided, and one of the essentials is to provide staff with clear instructions about what to do in the event of fire or other emergencies. Policy decisions on eating and drinking in the building are helpful, and account should be taken of the smoking ban now in place.

4.7.3   Listed buildings

Many charities work from listed buildings, which may provide a pleasant general environment but prove difficult to adapt as the charity expands (in view of the conflict between modern safety standards and the conservation interest). Security from theft or damage is also increasingly necessary, and may be difficult to reconcile with other considerations. Adaptations or special arrangements may be required where sensitive equipment is installed.

4.7.4   Moving premises

Moving premises, for example when a charity acquires its own premises for the first time, or when it decides to move to a different or cheaper location, brings its own opportunities and risks. Simple precautions, such as notifying regular contacts of the proposed change of address, should be planned well in advance and may provide a good occasion for a wider and more general mailshot.

Budgeting for the new premises is essential and in this process the longer-term, as well as the shorter-term, should be considered. For example, questions to be raised could be as follows: Should a reserve fund for future repairs and decorations be set up from the start? Will the existing equipment be sufficient? Will the new location enable savings to be made on incidental costs, for example can staff be recruited locally, saving on season ticket loans?

4.7.5   Neighbours

It is also useful to research the local services and facilities and to consider whether savings could be achieved or efficiency increased by co-operating with neighbours. It is most important that a charity should have good relations with its neighbours. Like any other business or resident, a charity is part of the local community and will be noticed and talked about. Good relations are vital where the activity of the charity is likely to cause concern to those living or working close by and who are not well-informed about how the charity operates. People who take the 'not in my backyard' approach and who object to activities they fear can often be pacified by a patient explanation of the purpose of the work, whether it is rehabilitation of drug users or the keeping of donkeys, and of the safeguards which the planners (presumably) have thought sufficient.

4.8 TRAINING

For some groups of people, regular training courses are taken for granted as a normal part of working life. For others, training does not seem relevant. For the latter group, training of the type given on a formal course may not be appropriate. However, there will undoubtedly be other forms of learning which they would welcome and enjoy. Included under the heading of 'training' for the purposes of this book are methods of learning connected directly or indirectly with the work of a charity.

Many trustees, employees and advisers of charities will have undergone professional or vocational training as part of their education. Most professions now require active members to undergo 'continuing education' to keep themselves up to date in a wide choice of subjects, some of which are very specialised. As a matter of interest, such formal courses include charity law for solicitors.

4.8.1 Self-help

In addition, individuals may gain access to further training opportunities by joining a professional association. For example, a lawyer who is interested may join the Charity Law Association or the Society of Trust and Estate Practitioners, and attend sociable meetings at which talks will be given. A chartered secretary may join the Charity Secretaries Group of the Institute of Chartered Secretaries and Administrators, which provides much the same benefits. A charity accountant may join the influential Charity Finance Directors' Group. Management training, as already noted, is widely available, whether at vast expense and prestige or through local authority courses for the voluntary sector or at some intermediate level or cost. Some so-called management courses are, unfortunately, eccentric or experimental and should not be tried by those of a nervous disposition. It is often better to start by joining an association of people performing similar work functions and decide, after discussion of the experiences of others, what course would be most suitable for an individual.

4.8.2 Academic institutions

Academic institutions are increasingly moving into the area of training for work with charities. For example, the London School of Economics and the City University (London) have relevant courses. The South Bank

University (also in London) has pioneered an MSc course in charity finance, and Exeter University includes a charities option in its MBA course.

4.8.3   Technical skills training

Training in technical skills is readily available at all levels of computing and other uses of information technology. In such a rapidly changing field, it is difficult for people honestly to claim that they know it all already.

4.8.4   Special courses

There are also courses designed with very particular types of students in mind, for example self-assertion for women.

4.8.5   Opportunities for staff

A good employer will encourage staff to undertake training courses whether by offering study leave or providing in-house training, but to make this worthwhile it is essential that the employee is given credit for the training undertaken and asked to make use of it. Charities need to have a policy on training.

One of the problems faced by junior staff or certain specialists is that they are categorised when they enter the charity's service and, in reality, have no opportunity of career development or diversification, except by leaving to go to another job. This is extremely wasteful of the very people whom a charity should be retaining and developing. It accords with the flexible spirit of most charities that such employees should be given better opportunities.

4.8.6   Informal training

Apart from formal training courses and organised professional activities there is a great deal of activity, within the charity world, in the sphere of informal learning through meetings and discussions. These can be of inestimable benefit not only to the participants themselves, whose problems at work will fall into perspective when compared with the experience of other people in similar posts, but also to the charity itself. Often at minimal cost, and during a lunch hour or in the early evening, those involved in running a charity can imbibe new ideas, gain in morale and bring back to the charity a sense of being part of a larger movement and of being near the forefront of the thinking within it.

Most of these meetings and discussions are advertised regularly by the NCVO or elsewhere in the charity press, and are attended not only by charity workers but also by trustees. There are many reasons why trustees should make more efforts to attend such meetings, both to learn and to contribute.

Following a small survey, which led to the announcement that a large proportion of charity trustees did not even know that they were trustees, the NCVO established a Trustee Training Unit, especially to help trustees to appreciate their responsibilities.

In-house training may sound more mundane, but there is certainly a place for a period of induction for new trustees, staff and volunteers, and there is no reason why these should not be combined to give the newcomers a chance to meet one another. There is also an advantage in getting staff and trustees together for conferences or meetings, or merely for social events, from time to time. It may also prove a useful and relatively painless method of bringing to light potential areas of conflict, and enable preventative or remedial action to be taken promptly. In addition, there may be scope for specialist training where the charity runs an institution, performs an unusual function, or has particular traditions which involve special ways of doing things.

For some charities, it may be economical, and provide additional interest for participants, to arrange a combined training activity with another charity, or another branch of the same charity, or with another organisation in the locality.

Learning and training should be an enjoyable, positive experience. It should also help to bind participants together, to facilitate co-operation and team-building and to reinforce the concept of belonging to the organisation and 'owning' its policies. It is therefore desirable to seek the best training available. On the other hand, it has cost implications and charities must be wary of extravagance. A constructive approach is to regard the cost as equivalent to an investment and to be careful both about initial selection and monitoring and utilising the service which has been provided.

4.9   TROUBLESHOOTING

No charity, however well-run, is immune from the occasional disaster or hitch. The importance lies in what is done about it and what is learned from it. Any action taken determines the degree to which the charity's credibility is damaged, and even whether or not the charity survives. Loss of credibility does not only mean loss of potential for fundraising; it can also make it difficult to recruit good staff or trustees or to be taken seriously by the authorities and others whom the charity wishes to reach.

4.9.1   Physical emergencies

Physical emergencies can be dealt with by practical steps, for example by having well-thought-out procedures to deal with fire or flood, and adequate insurance cover.

4.9.2   Insurance

Insurance will also go some way to assist in the case of financial loss through negligence or theft or other dishonesty on the part of members of staff, although careful selection procedures, including the taking-up of references and prudent financial management which avoids putting temptation in people's way, is preferable and usually effective.

4.9.3   Negligence

Losses caused by the negligence of advisers or other independent contractors should be recoverable from their professional indemnity insurers, if necessary through court action. This is one of the arguments in favour of appointing a surveyor or architect to supervise work on a building project.

4.9.4   Tenants' defaults

The defaults of tenants who are not beneficiaries of the charity can be guarded against by taking adequate deposits on the grant of the tenancy, making sure that there is an effective system for collecting rent and investigating every suspected breach of covenant.

4.9.5   Compensation

Failures by suppliers or service-providers can be dealt with by a claim for compensation. Similarly, if a trustee wanders off the straight and narrow and commits a breach of trust, prompt action, if necessary through the courts, will often provide the best solution.

4.9.6   Problems

Troubleshooting is less straightforward in three sets of circumstances, outlined below.

4.9.6.1   *Running out of money*

A charity which has made plans on the strength of promises of money which do not materialise may find it impossible to continue to operate on anything like the scale it envisaged, and may be forced to make staff redundant or even to wind up the charity. In the case of a charitable company, the charity trustees will be personally at risk of having to pay the charity's debts if they allow it to continue operating while it is technically insolvent (ie cannot pay its debts from its assets). It *must*, therefore, stop operations.

It is wise to cease operating in such circumstances even where company law does not provide this incentive. It is then up to the trustees to take urgent steps either to find the required funds or to reorganise the charity's work in a way which is practicable. It may involve a radical alteration to the constitution or functions of the charity, or amalgamation with a similar charity, or even a takeover by another body of trustees.

If a charity is vulnerable through dependence on grant aid, the staff must be made aware of this, and sufficient financial advice should be obtained in order that staff and beneficiaries may be protected as far as possible. This is also another very good reason for maintaining co-operative relationships with other bodies.

4.9.6.2 *Charity Commission inquiry (England and Wales)*

Anyone may make a complaint about a particular charity to the Charity Commission, who have the staff and resources to investigate any complaint which is well-founded and does not refer to an exempt charity or a charity outside England and Wales. There are other bodies (such as the Housing Corporation) which will investigate complaints against specific types of exempt charity.

The Commission have a number of wide-ranging powers to protect the assets of a charity which is under investigation and may, for example, obtain information and documents, order a professional audit, suspend trustees and officers, freeze bank accounts and prevent transactions with the charity even before their investigation is complete. Subsequently, they may decide to remove one or more of the trustees or officers, appoint new trustees, appoint a receiver and manager to run the charity or even transfer the assets to another charity and wind up the original charity (in the case of a charitable company, they petition the court to do so). Further, the Commission or the Attorney-General may decide to bring legal proceedings against one or more of the trustees, seeking to make them personally liable for the damage to the charity. In obvious cases the Commission may order a trustee to make restoration to the charity without the need for legal proceedings.

A relaxation in the confidentiality principles allows HM Revenue and Customs ('HMRC'), rating authorities and others to share their information with the Commission when there is reason to suspect abuse.

Although a large proportion of the complaints investigated ultimately prove unfounded, the fact that a charity is being investigated, which is frequently of interest to the press, grant-makers and others, tends to indicate that something is wrong with the charity or its administration and this, in itself, can be very damaging.

To avoid uncalled for complaints, charity trustees should, first, take care not to do anything which would allow staff, tenants, advisers or beneficiaries to feel that they have been unfairly treated, and internal complaints procedures should be established to deal with such problems. Regrettably, there are occasions when the director or other senior staff member has become alienated from the trustees and, despite the risk to his or her job, will take a perceived problem to the Commission instead of consulting the trustees. Secondly, it is prudent to establish good relationships with the press, by providing ample information and responding helpfully when asked.

If a serious complaint is made or a formal investigation is proposed, one of the most constructive responses, which will generally be welcomed by the Commission, is for the charity to set up its own inquiry to establish the facts and correct and learn from any mistakes which have been made. This is not only very helpful and positive in itself, but enables any press reports to sound positive, and underlines the fact that the trustees, not the disaster, are in charge.

4.9.6.3   *Lord Advocate's powers (Scotland)*

Similar powers can be exercised in relation to Scottish charities by the Court of Session. If satisfied that there has been misconduct or mismanagement in the running of a Scottish charity, the Lord Advocate, whose functions parallel those of the Attorney-General in relation to charities in England and Wales, may make an application to the Court of Session seeking an appropriate remedy such as the removal of a trustee or the making of a scheme.

4.9.7   Mediation

Nevertheless, it is a regrettable fact that many charities suffer, from time to time, from internal disputes, either within the workforce or the trustee body or between one and the other. There is no reasonable excuse for such self-defeating and destructive behaviour, which fits no one's idea of charity.

Publicity is extremely damaging in this situation, both because it encourages attitudes to harden and because of its effect on the charity's public image.

Good management, open communications, the careful selection of trustees and staff, a strong sense of commitment and agreed priorities will all help to guard against this kind of calamity. If it does arise, however, feelings are likely to run high, righteous indignation flourishes and intemperate words may appear in print.

The best solution is *not* to complain of maladministration to the Charity Commission or the Office of the Scottish Charity Regulator ('OSCR') (although they may sometimes be able to suggest a solution) or to resort to litigation (although for some disputes this can appear to be the only way to decide the matter) but to try to resolve the matter amicably in the interests of the charity by negotiation or other means.

The use of alternative dispute resolution ('ADR') is now accepted as a preferred course to litigation and involves a series of techniques aimed at finding solutions without recourse to the courts. Arbitration is one method, but tends to be costly. Another, less expensive and, in many ways, more satisfactory, technique is mediation. A mediator, preferably someone who has been specially trained in the method and who may be nominated by an independent outside agency, is appointed to assist the parties to reach a solution by agreement. The mediator's fees are paid equally by both sides to ensure impartiality. The process is not binding unless and until an agreement is reached. The mediator will not impose the solution but try to bring out the underlying common ground between the parties and discover in what ways the matters which they regard as most important can be incorporated into the solution. Most mediations result in a final, binding agreement, and those which do not often make the remaining stages in the dispute simpler and easier to deal with.

CHAPTER 5

EUROPE

5.1 HOW CHARITIES FIT IN

There are equivalents of charities in other European countries, but since their legal systems are based on Roman law, which did not have the need to develop the trust concept or the concept of charitable purposes, English law stands out as having the most developed legal concept of charity and the most refined methods of supervision and accountability. In relation to what we recognise as charities, the technical form of the organisation is far more important in Europe than in this country. In Europe, two main categories are prevalent: *foundations*, which are similar to UK charitable trusts but have a corporate form; and *associations*, which are similar to what would be called voluntary organisations in the UK. In addition, churches in Europe carry out a good deal of charitable work directly.

The European Union ('EU') has only recently begun to come to grips with the voluntary sector in general. For many years it was regarded as having little relevance to the European economy and outside (what used to be called) the Common Market. That view has been modified with the recognition that 'not-for-profit' bodies have an effect on the economy as users and providers of services, that social questions are highly relevant to economic results and that the voluntary sector has grown and continues to do so. As a result, the expression 'social economy' or 'l'économie sociale' has been coined.

5.1.1 Social economy

The social economy covers much more than charitable purposes or organisations. It includes non-charitable friendly societies, agricultural co-operatives and other mutual trading bodies, housing associations and what is known as 'social tourism', ie the provision of holidays for workers or for the poor. Such organisations may operate in commercial ways, except that their aim is not profit but the benefit of members or a section of the public. They are sometimes designated, in French, organisations 'sans but lucratif', a phrase which is closer in meaning to 'non-profit-distributing', or the American phrase 'not-for-profit' than to the usually inexact 'non-profit-making'.

At present, Europe-wide regulation of the social economy is in inchoate form, and it may be many years before decisions are taken and implemented to either harmonise the rules (including supervision on the one hand and tax reliefs on the other) between Member States or, bearing in mind the emergence of the principle of subsidiarity, to leave most of these matters to individual States to regulate in accordance with their national cultural traditions. Regulations designed to prevent money laundering and funds being used for terrorist purposes are in place. On the other hand, the issue of whether, and if so how, to operate in other European countries and to tap European sources of funds, will be of increasing relevance to charities which are not purely local (and even to some which are) as the EU encroaches on more aspects of life.

5.2   EUROPEAN LAW

As a result of being a signatory to the European treaties, the UK is subject to EU law, which must be applied by UK courts. There are, however, different kinds of EU legislation which affect us in different ways.

5.2.1   Treaties

The treaties, which may be amended and supplemented from time to time, are the primary legislation and directly applicable to governments and commercial (and other) entities. They define the areas of policy for which the Community is responsible and set out general principles, for example on competition, which can have a direct effect on the way economic activities operate. The Maastricht Treaty (which came into force on 1 November 1993) established the European Union. This has since been amended by later treaties.

5.2.2   Regulations

Regulations are binding, unavoidable and directly applicable in the courts of all Member States.

5.2.3   Directives

Directives are addressed to national governments and require them to introduce domestic legislation to achieve a stated result. The method of achieving that stated result is for the individual Member State to decide. Directives are, naturally, less detailed than regulations and deal with policy. However, they are binding on the Member States, who must report what steps have been taken to implement them and do so by a specified date.

5.2.4 Decisions

Decisions are addressed to particular Member States, institutions or individuals, on whom they are binding.

5.2.5 Recommendations and Opinions

Recommendations and Opinions are not binding but, nevertheless, carry considerable weight, and may be referred to in decisions of the European Court of Justice.

5.3 EUROPEAN INSTITUTIONS

There is an interlocking series of institutions which carry out the functions of the EU in ways which are still being refined and developed.

The following summary of the European institutions explains by which of the institutions the foregoing expressions of the authority of the EU are made.

5.3.1 Council of Ministers

The Council of Ministers is the principal legislative assembly and, whilst it was originally intended to legislate only on proposals from the Commission (see below), it has taken on the role of initiating policy. This is of particular relevance in enlarging the scope of Community policy where the subject is not clearly covered by the treaties. Whilst there are 27 national ministers (one per member state), the composition of the Council depends on the question at issue. Thus, at a General Council meeting the Foreign Ministers of Member States will be present, whereas more specialised ministers will attend meetings of the Technical Councils, dealing with such matters as agriculture. The President of the Council of Ministers is often referred to as the President of the Union, a post which is held by Member States, in turn, for six months at a time, and enables the holder to set the agenda.

5.3.2 Committees of Permanent Representatives

Preparatory work for meetings of the Council of Ministers is carried out by one of the Committees of Permanent Representatives ('COREPERS 1 and 2') and, below them, by a number of committees and working parties which advise the Council and Commission and analyse Commission proposals. There is also an informal group of committees advising on policy areas which are not formally covered by the treaties.

5.3.3   European Council

The European Council is not provided for under the treaties but has developed in response to a need. It consists of the heads of government of the Member States and the heads of the Commission, who aim to set goals and make policy decisions (sometimes on specific issues), consider the admission of new members to the Community, resolve internal problems and deal with challenges which face the Community from outside. Meetings are held at least every six months.

5.3.4   Commission

The Commission is often described as the Civil Service of the EU but, whilst it has equivalent functions, it has greater influence and power to initiate policy than a government department in the UK. It is headed by 27 Commissioners (one per member state), each with responsibility for a particular area of policy allocated by the President of the Commission, who is appointed by the European Council with the approval of the European Parliament. Each Commissioner is supported by a 'cabinet' of officials, usually from his or her own Member State.

5.3.5   Directorates General

Below the Commissioners are the Directorates General, whose responsibilities are concerned with different areas of policy. The social economy comes under Directorate General 23 (usually referred to as DG XXIII), a small Directorate General with only two directorates and no divisions within it.

There have been problems when issues cut across the policy areas of more than one Directorate General which have affected those in the voluntary sector. A provisional consultative committee has been set up to ensure that the Commission takes account of the effects on charities and kindred bodies when drawing up legislation. Those functions of the Commission which are of most concern to charities are described under 'Interaction' at **5.4** below.

5.3.6   European Parliament

The European Parliament is a directly elected assembly whose members sit for terms of five years. At present there are 785 MEPs (although this is due to change under the Treaty of Lisbon). Members gravitate to various groups, according to their national party, the most prominent of which are the European People's Party (roughly 'Christian Democrat') and the

Socialist Group. There is also the Alliance of Liberals and Democrats for Europe, the Group of the Greens and the Group for the European Unitarian Left. The procedural arrangements make provision for representation of the various groupings, both in plenary sessions and in committees.

The plenary sessions take place in Strasbourg and the committees meet in Brussels. The secretariat is based in Luxembourg, where the library is situated. Researchers and parliamentary staff make use of the library for information on social issues, to which charities may usefully contribute material.

The main functions of the European Parliament are the consideration of proposed legislation via the committees (see below) and, most importantly, the setting of the budget. The European Parliament is able to suggest amendments to legislative proposals and to add new areas of expenditure to the budget. If, when so doing, it oversteps the limits of the areas for which there is formal authority to operate, it is understood that the Commission and the Council of Ministers will provide the necessary authority. Areas of particular interest to charities are mentioned under 'Interaction' at **5.4** below.

5.3.7   Committees

The committees carry out most of the work of the Parliament. There are 20 permanent committees and several ad hoc committees which are formed to consider specific issues. The concerns of charities are not covered by any one committee but are distributed between several, including the standing committees for Social Affairs, Employment and the Working Environment and for Agriculture, Fisheries and Rural Development. The committees examine proposals from the Commission on which the opinion of Parliament is sought, and each is led by a 'rapporteur'.

5.3.8   Economic and Social Committee

The Economic and Social Committee ('ECOSOC') consists of 222 members chosen by the governments of Member States and representing three main groups – employers, workers and others (including environmental protection agencies, the professions, small businesses, consumers and local authorities). This committee was established because it was considered that the European Parliament did not provide enough scope for the discussion of these specific interests. The Committee is divided into nine sections, dealing, for example, with the environment, public health, social issues, family issues and educational and cultural matters. There is a plenary session in Brussels 10 or 12 times a year, and the Committee gives influential Opinions, prepared by rapporteurs after careful consultation, on EU affairs.

Referral of a question to the Committee for its Opinion is sometimes compulsory, in cases where it concerns social policy or the European Social Fund, but is otherwise optional. The Committee may also give an Opinion on its own initiative.

5.3.9   Committee of the Regions

The Committee of the Regions was established in 1994 by the Maastricht Treaty. It represents regional interests and is composed of 244 representatives of local governments.

5.3.10   European Foundation

The European Foundation for the Improvement of Living and Working Conditions, usually referred to as just the European Foundation, is based in Dublin. Its members represent employers, trade unions and governments. The Foundation produces detailed reports on major issues, including, for example, housing projects for the young and counselling for the long-term unemployed, and also holds conferences on particular themes.

5.3.11   Council of Europe

The Council of Europe is not an institution of the European Community but was set up after the Second World War to safeguard the cultural heritage of the European peoples, especially respect for human rights and the rule of law by democratic institutions, and to encourage social and economic progress.

It consists of a Committee of Ministers and a Parliamentary Assembly, both drawn from the democratic institutions in European countries, and a Standing Conference of Local and Regional Authorities. It was the first body in Europe to recognise the need for consultation arrangements for non-governmental organisations ('NGOs') (see **5.4.5** below).

5.4   INTERACTION

It can truly be said that making positive use of the European institutions and obtaining grants from them is an art in itself. The following may help to indicate areas which are worth exploring.

5.4.1   Commission

To influence Community legislation and the adoption of new policies the best approach may be via the Commission, which, in formulating legislative and policy proposals, has a healthy tradition of consulting people and organisations which have expertise in the subject, and setting up committees for this purpose. In 2000 an autonomous European Standing Conference of Co-operatives, Mutual Societies, Associations and Foundations (CEP-CMAF) was created to replace the previous consultative committee. It provides a forum for discussion with the Commission of general matters affecting bodies within the social economy and gives these organisations better visibility at a political level.

The Commission also monitors Community policy and supervises its implementation, by making decisions, regulations and directives, ensuring consistency and collecting (and spending) revenue (for example VAT). There are two 'structural funds' of particular relevance to charities from which it is possible to obtain grant aid. The European Social Fund and the European Regional Development Fund operate in a co-ordinated way to achieve five aims:

(1)   to develop backward regions;

(2)   to change declining industrial areas;

(3)   to integrate the young into the job market;

(4)   to deal with long-term unemployment; and

(5)   to develop rural areas.

In addition, there are 'Community Initiatives' and various other programmes of relevance to charities which aim to promote a more balanced economic and social development.

The Commission shares with the European Court of Justice the role of ensuring compliance with Community legislation, for example failures on the part of national governments to implement directives.

5.4.2   European Parliament

As indicated above, the European Parliament is a true debating assembly and not a legislature. Its major decision-making concern is the budget. Indirect influence through the library at Luxembourg has already been mentioned (see **5.3.6** above).

It is also possible to influence ultimate decision-making by persuading an MEP to suggest amendments to proposed legislation which comes to the Parliament for its opinion before being laid before the Council of Ministers. Less commonly, the Parliament is given the opportunity of the equivalent of a second reading of a proposal after the Council of Ministers has considered it, or may be consulted on a policy issue even before a proposal is formulated.

5.4.3   European Social Committee

The European Social Committee is not a decision-making body, but it does exercise a serious influence on policy and may be persuaded to recruit expert advisers from charities operating in the field which it is considering, or to incorporate, in its reports, information or materials produced by relevant charities.

5.4.4   European Foundation

Similar influences may be possible in relation to European Foundation reports. Attendance at a conference may also prove very helpful in establishing contacts for the charity with others concerned with similar problems.

5.4.5   Non-governmental organisations

The work of the Council of Europe with NGOs has led to increased influence for these bodies, which must be international. They can apply to be consulted in any of nine fields, including health, youth, heritage and the environment and human rights, and act as advisers to the Council or its committees and through various NGO meetings and networks. A charity which is not itself an international body can gain influence indirectly through one which is.

5.4.6   European programmes

In addition to the European Foundation, there is another permanent agency, the European Centre for Vocational Training ('CEDEFOP') which is relevant to the work of some charities.

Besides these permanent groups there is a series of short-term programmes in the field of social policy which provide either funds or information and advice, or a combination, and report back to the Directorate General by which they were established. The programmes are operated through existing outside agencies, many of which have advisory committees which provide another avenue of influence for interested charities.

Among these programmes are specialised regional or local networks combating poverty, which have been in existence with more or less similar aims since the 1970s. Charities are usually closely involved with such work, and efforts are made by means of research projects and otherwise to build on the experience gained and pass on the lessons learned. There is a research project based at the Warwick Business School which supports the programme in the UK. The central control is based in Lille, France and there is a liaison committee between the Commission and the national governments which, in the UK, includes a representative from the Department for Work and Pensions.

5.5 NETWORKS AND UMBRELLA BODIES

See Appendix C: Official Addresses.

There is an enormous proliferation of networking bodies which operate throughout Europe and, for most charities, they provide the ideal way to examine ways of both operating directly and gaining useful knowledge from other European countries. Some of the more major are listed below:

(1) The National Council for Voluntary Organisations ('NCVO') in the UK provides very practical guidance to member organisations on how and with whom to make contact, on networking and how to apply for grant aid. It aims to act as spokesman, in Europe and in Westminster and Whitehall, for the voluntary sector generally.

(2) The Comité Européen des Associations d'Intérêt Général ('CEDAG') is a network emanating originally from the Council of Europe, which is leading moves for more formal arrangements within the Community for consultation with charities and other voluntary bodies. There is a proposed European Association Statute on which CEDAG has for some years been in discussion with the Commission, via DG XXIII (see **5.3.5** above). Among other things, these would give legal personality to a 'European Association'. A White Paper on associations and foundations in the EU is also planned. This will be concerned with their contribution to the social economy and may make recommendations for improving their regulation and financing.

(3) In addition, CEDAG uses its influence to press for funding for charitable work and has helped to establish an interest group for the sector (known as the Social Economy Intergroup) within the European Parliament. This is likely to provide an effective means of enabling charities, and the voluntary sector generally, to make members of the European Parliament aware of the issues which affect the sector.

(4) The European Foundation Centre ('EFC') represents grant-making bodies across Europe and has links with the Association of Charitable Foundations in the UK and, less directly, with the Council on Foundations in the USA.

(5) The International Society for Third Sector Research ('ISTR') has been established to promote academic research and teaching concerning 'the third, voluntary or non-profit sector' on an international basis.

5.6   RECENT DEVELOPMENTS IN EU LAW RELATING TO CHARITIES

5.6.1   EC Consultation

In 2005 the European Commission consulted member states on a draft code of conduct for non-profit organisations to promote transparency and accountability best practices. The resulting guidelines were specifically aimed at preventing the exploitation of organisations for the financing of terrorism, in particular Special Recommendation VIII adopted by the Financial Action Task Force states that countries 'should address the vulnerabilities of the non-profit sector'.

5.6.2   Cross-border charitable giving

On 14 September 2006 the ECJ gave its ruling in the case of Centro di Musicologia Walter Stauffer v Finanzamt Munchen fur Korperschaften (Case C-386/04). The ECJ ruled that it was contrary to the EC Treaty for member states to only give tax relief to charitable foundations established in that particular member state and to refuse to grant the same exemption in relation to similar income to a charitable foundation solely on the ground that it had been established in another member state.

APPENDIX A

MODEL DOCUMENTS

A1   Charity Law Association: Model Trust Deed for a Charitable Trust (2nd Edition)

THIS TRUST DEED made	[*date*] by the First Trustees:

(1) _____

_____

(2) _____

_____

(3) _____

[*full names and residential addresses of all of the First Trustees*]

WITNESSES AS FOLLOWS

1.   INTRODUCTION

1.1   The First Trustees hold *[details]* on the trusts declared in this Deed.

1.2   Further money or property may be paid or transferred to the **Trustees** for the **Charity**.

1.3   [any other explanatory statement]

2.   NAME & OBJECTS

2.1   The name of the Charity is *[NAME]* (or any other name chosen by resolution of the Trustees).

2.2   The **Objects** are *[OBJECTS]*.

2.3   The Trustees must use the income [and may use the capital] of the Charity in promoting the Objects.

3.   POWERS
The Trustees have the following powers, which may be exercised only in promoting the Objects:

3.1   To promote or carry out research.

3.2   To provide advice.

3.3   To publish or distribute information.

3.4 To co-operate with other bodies.

3.5 To support, administer or set up other charities.

3.6 To raise funds (but not by means of **taxable trading**).

3.7 To borrow money and give security for loans (but only in accordance with the restrictions imposed by the **Charities Act**).

3.8 To acquire or hire property of any kind.

3.9 To let or dispose of property of any kind (but only in accordance with the restrictions imposed by the Charities Act).

3.10 To make grants or loans of money and to give guarantees.

3.11 To set aside funds for special purposes or as reserves against future expenditure.

3.12 [To deposit or invest funds in any manner (but to invest only after obtaining such advice from a **financial expert** as the Trustees consider necessary and having regard to the suitability of investments and the need for diversification).]

3.13 [To delegate the management of investments to a financial expert, but only on terms that:
   (1) the investment policy is recorded **in writing** for the financial expert by the Trustees;
   (2) every transaction is reported promptly to the Trustees;
   (3) the performance of the investments is reviewed regularly with the Trustees;
   (4) the Trustees are entitled to cancel the delegation arrangement at any time;
   (5) the investment policy and the delegation arrangement are reviewed at least once a **year**;
   (6) all payments due to the financial expert are on a scale or at a level which is agreed in advance and are reported promptly to the Trustees on receipt;
   (7) the financial expert must not do anything outside the powers of the Trustees.]

3.14 To insure the property of the Charity against any foreseeable risk and take out other insurance policies to protect the Charity when required.

3.15 To pay for **indemnity insurance** for the Trustees.

3.16 Subject to clause 6.3, to employ paid or unpaid agents, staff or advisers.

3.17 To enter into contracts to provide services to or on behalf of other bodies.

3.18 To establish or acquire subsidiary companies to assist or act as agents for the Charity.

3.19 To pay the costs of forming the Charity.

3.20 To do anything else within the law which promotes or helps to promote the Objects.

4.   THE TRUSTEES

4.1   The Trustees as **charity trustees** have control of the Charity and its property and funds.

4.2   The full number of Trustees is [three] individuals [who *add any special qualifications*].

4.3   Subject to clause 4.7, the First Trustees [are entitled to hold office for life] [are entitled to hold office for the following periods from the date of this Deed:

Trustee's name]	*[Number] years*
[Trustee's name]	*[Number] years*
[Trustee's name]	*[Number] years].*

4.4   Future Trustees must be appointed [for terms of office of *[number]* years] by resolution of the Trustees.

4.5   [A retiring Trustee who is competent to act may be re-appointed at the end of the term of office [but a Trustee is not eligible for re-appointment until *[number]* year[s] after *[number]* consecutive terms of office.]

4.6   Every future Trustee must sign a declaration of willingness to act as a Trustee of the Charity before he or she may vote at any meeting of the Trustees.

4.7   A Trustee automatically ceases to be a Trustee if he or she:
      (1)   is disqualified under the Charities Act from acting as a charity trustee or trustee for a charity;

(2) is incapable, whether mentally or physically, of managing his/her own affairs;

(3) is absent [without notice] from *[number]* consecutive meetings of Trustees [and is asked by a majority of the other Trustees to resign];

(4) resigns by **written** notice to the Trustees (but only if at least two Trustees will remain in office);

(5) [ceases to be [specially qualified];]

(6) [is removed by a resolution passed by all the other Trustees after they have invited the views of the Trustee concerned and considered the matter in the light of any such views.]

4.8 A retiring Trustee is entitled [on written request] to an indemnity from the continuing Trustees at the expense of the Charity in respect of any liabilities properly incurred during his/her trusteeship.

4.9 A technical defect in the appointment of a Trustee of which the Trustees are unaware at the time does not invalidate decisions taken by the Trustees.

5. PROCEEDINGS OF TRUSTEES

5.1 The Trustees must hold at least *[number]* meetings each year.

5.2 A quorum at a meeting of the Trustees is *[number]* Trustees.

5.3 [A meeting may be held either in person or by suitable electronic means agreed by the Trustees in which all participants may communicate with all the other participants.]

5.4 The **[Chairman]** or (if the Chairman is unable or unwilling to do so) some other Trustee chosen by them presides at each meeting of the Trustees.

5.5 Except where otherwise provided in this Deed, every issue may be determined by a simple majority of the votes cast at a meeting of the Trustees but a resolution which is in writing and signed by all the Trustees is as valid as a resolution passed at a meeting. For this purpose the resolution may be contained in more than one document and will be treated as passed on the date of the last signature.

5.6 Except for the chairman of the meeting, who has a [second or] casting vote, every Trustee has one vote on each issue.

5.7 A procedural defect of which the Trustees are unaware at the time does not invalidate decisions taken at a meeting of the Trustees.

6.   ADMINISTRATIVE POWERS OF TRUSTEES
The Trustees have the following powers in the administration of the Charity:

6.1   To appoint the Chairman, a Treasurer and any other honorary officers from among their number.

6.2   [To delegate any of their functions to committees consisting of two or more persons appointed by them (but at least [two] members of every committee must be Trustees and all proceedings of committees must be reported promptly to the Trustees).]

6.3   To make rules consistent with this Deed to govern their proceedings and proceedings of committees.

6.4   To make regulations consistent with this Deed to govern the administration of the Charity including the use and application of the [income] [property and funds] the operation of bank accounts and the commitment of funds).

7.   BENEFITS TO TRUSTEES

7.1   The property and funds of the Charity must only be used for promoting the Objects and do not belong to the Trustees.

7.2   No Trustee may receive any payment of money or other **material benefit** (whether direct or indirect) from the Charity except:
      (1)   under clause[s] 3.15 (indemnity insurance) [and 7.3 (contractual payments)];
      (2)   reimbursement of reasonable out-of-pocket expenses (including authorised hotel and travel costs) actually incurred in the administration of the Charity;
      (3)   interest at a reasonable rate on money lent to the Charity;
      (4)   a reasonable rent or hiring fee for property let or hired to the Charity;
      (5)   an indemnity in respect of any liabilities properly incurred in the running the Charity (including the costs of a successful defence to criminal proceedings);
      (6)   payment to a company in which the Trustee has no more than a 1 per cent shareholding;
      (7)   in exceptional cases, other payments or benefits (but only with the written approval of the **Commission** in advance).

7.3   A Trustee may not be an employee of the Charity[, but a Trustee or any **connected person** may enter into a contract with the Trustees to supply goods or services in return for a payment or other **material benefit** but only if:
      (1)   the goods or services are actually required for the Charity;

(2) the nature and level of the benefit is no more than reasonable in relation to the value of the goods or services and is set at a meeting of the Trustees in accordance with the procedure in clause 7.4; and

(3) not more than *[number or proportion up to one half]* of the Trustees are interested in such a contract in any one **financial year**.]

7.4 Whenever a Trustee has a personal interest in a matter to be discussed at a meeting of the Trustees or any committee, the Trustee concerned must:

(1) declare an interest before the meeting or at the meeting before discussion on the matter begins;

(2) be absent from the meeting for that item unless expressly invited to remain in order to provide information;

(3) not be counted in the quorum during that part of the meeting;

(4) be absent during the vote and have no vote on the matter.

8. PROPERTY AND FUNDS

8.1 Funds which are not required for immediate use (including those which will be required for use at a future date) must be placed on deposit or invested [in accordance with clause 3.12] until needed.

8.2 Investments and other property of the Charity may be held:

(1) in the names of the Trustees (or in the name of the trustee body if incorporated under the Charities Act);

(2) [in the name of a **nominee company** acting under the control of the Trustees or of a financial expert acting under their instructions;]

(3) in the name of a **trust corporation** as a **holding trustee** for the Charity which must be appointed (and may be removed) by deed executed by the Trustees;

(4) in the case of land, by the Official Custodian for Charities under an order of the Commission or the Court.

8.3 [Documents and physical assets may be deposited with any company registered or having a place of business in England and Wales as **custodian**.]

8.4 [Any [nominee company acting under clause 8.2(2), [and] [any trust corporation appointed under clause 8.2(3)] [and any custodian appointed under clause 8.3] may be paid reasonable fees.]

9. RECORDS & ACCOUNTS

9.1 The Trustees must comply with the requirements of the Charities Act as to the keeping of financial records, the audit or independent examination of the accounts and the preparation and transmission to the Commission of:
(1)   annual returns;
(2)   annual reports; and
(3)   annual statements of account.

9.2 The Trustees must maintain proper records of:
(1)   all proceedings at meetings of the Trustees;
(2)   all reports of committees; and
(3)   all professional advice obtained.

9.3 Accounting records relating to the Charity must be made available for inspection by any Trustee at any time during normal office hours.

9.4 A copy of the Charity's latest available statement of account must be supplied on request to any Trustee. A copy must also be supplied, within two **months**, to any person who makes a written request and pays the Charity's reasonable costs.

10.   [AMENDMENTS
This Deed may be amended by supplemental deed on a resolution passed by *[proportion]* of the Trustees but:

10.1 No amendment is valid if it would make a **fundamental change** to the Objects or to this clause or destroy the charitable status of the Charity.

10.2 Clause 7 may not be amended without the prior written consent of the Commission.]

11.   [AMALGAMATION

11.1 The Trustees may at any time on a resolution passed by at least *[proportion]* of the Trustees transfer the assets and liabilities of the Charity to another charity established for exclusively charitable purposes within, the same as or similar to the Objects [and which *add any special condition*].

11.2 On a transfer under clause 11.1 the Trustees must ensure that all necessary steps are taken as to:
(1)   the transfer of land and other property;
(2)   the novation of contracts of employment and the transfer of any pension rights; and
(3)   the trusteeship of any property held for special purposes.]

12.   [DISSOLUTION

12.1 The Trustees may at any time decide by resolution passed by [at least *proportion*] of the Trustees that the Charity is to be dissolved. The Trustees will then be responsible for the orderly winding up of the Charity's affairs.

12.2 After making provision for all outstanding liabilities of the Charity, the Trustees must apply the remaining property and funds in one or more of the following ways:
   (1) by transfer to one or more other bodies established for exclusively charitable purposes within, the same as or similar to the Objects;
   (2) directly for the Objects or charitable purposes within or similar to the Objects; or
   (3) in such other manner consistent with charitable status as the Commission approve in writing in advance.

12.3 A final report and statement of account relating to the Charity must be sent to the Commission.]

13. INTERPRETATION
In this Deed:

13.1 The following expressions have the following meanings:

['area of benefit' means *[geographical area]*;]
['beneficiaries:' means *[qualifications of beneficiaries]*;]
['the Chairman'] means the person appointed by the Trustees to preside at their meetings;
'the Charities Act' means the Charities Act 1993;
'the Charity' means the charitable trust created and governed by this Deed;
'charity trustees' has the meaning prescribed by section 97(1) of the Charities Act;
'the Commission' means the Charity Commissioners for England and Wales;
'connected person' means any spouse, partner, brother, sister, child, parent, grandchild or grandparent of a Trustee, any **firm** of which a Trustee is a member or employee and any company of which a Trustee is a director, employee or shareholder having a beneficial interest in more than 1 per cent of the share capital;
['custodian' has the meaning prescribed by section 17(2) of the Trustee Act 2000;]
['financial expert' means an individual, company or firm who is authorised to give investment advice under the Financial Services and Markets Act 2000;]
['financial year' means the Charity's financial year;]
'the First Trustees' means the parties to this Deed;
'firm' includes a limited liability partnership;

['fundamental change' means such a change as would not have been within the reasonable contemplation of a person making a donation to the Charity;]

'holding trustee' means an individual or corporate body responsible for holding the title to property but not authorised to make any decisions relating to its use, investment or disposal;

'indemnity insurance' means insurance against personal liability incurred by any Trustee for an act or omission which is or is alleged to be a breach of trust or breach of duty, unless the Trustee concerned knew that, or was reckless whether, the act or omission was a breach of trust or breach of duty.

'independent examination' has the meaning prescribed by section 43(3)(a) of the Charities Act;

'material benefit' means a benefit which may not be financial but has a monetary value;

'month' means calendar month;

['nominee company' means a corporate body registered or having a place of business in England and Wales;]

'the Objects' means the charitable objects set out in clause 2;

'taxable trading' means carrying on a trade or business for the principal purpose of raising funds, and not for the purpose of actually carrying out the Objects, the profits of which are liable to income or corporation tax;

'trust corporation' has the meaning prescribed by section 205(1)(xxviii) of the Law of Property Act 1925 but does not include the Public Trustee;

'Trustee' means a trustee of the Charity and Trustees means the trustees of the Charity;

'written' or 'in writing' refers to a legible document on paper [not] including a fax message;

'year' means calendar year;

13.2 References to an Act of Parliament are references to the Act as amended or re-enacted from time to time and to any subordinate legislation made under it.

IN WITNESS of the above the parties have executed this Deed

SIGNED AS A DEED BY

_____   _____

[*Name of Trustee*]   [*Signature of Trustee*]
in the presence of:

_____

_____

[*Name, address and occupation of witness*]

[*Signature of Witness*]

[*Repeat for each of the Trustees*]

A2 Charity Law Association: Model Memorandum and Articles of Association for a Charitable Company (2nd Edition)

COMPANIES ACTS 1985 AND 1989
COMPANY LIMITED BY GUARANTEE

MEMORANDUM OF ASSOCIATION OF

_____ *[name]*

1. **NAME**
   The name of the **Charity** is *[NAME]*.

2. **REGISTERED OFFICE**
   The registered office of the Charity is to be in England and Wales.

3. **OBJECTS**

The objects of the Charity are _____

_____

_____

_____

_____

_____

_____ *[objects]* ('**the Objects**').

4. **POWERS**
   The Charity has the following powers, which may be exercised only in promoting the Objects:

4.1 To promote or carry out research.

4.2 To provide advice.

4.3 To publish or distribute information.

4.4 To co-operate with other bodies.

4.5 To support, administer or set up other charities.

4.6 To raise funds (but not by means of **taxable trading**).

4.7 To borrow money and give security for loans (but only in accordance with the restrictions imposed by the **Charities Act**).

4.8 To acquire or hire property of any kind.

4.9 To let or dispose of property of any kind (but only in accordance with the restrictions imposed by the Charities Act).

4.10 To make grants or loans of money and to give guarantees.

4.11 To set aside funds for special purposes or as reserves against future expenditure.

4.12 To deposit or invest in funds in any manner (but to invest only after obtaining such advice from a **financial expert** as the **Trustees** consider necessary and having regard to the suitability of investments and the need for diversification).

4.13 To delegate the management of investments to a financial expert, but only on terms that:
    (1)   the investment policy is set down **in writing** for the financial expert by the Trustees;
    (2)   every transaction is reported promptly to the Trustees;
    (3)   the performance of the investments is reviewed regularly with the Trustees;
    (4)   the Trustees are entitled to cancel the delegation arrangement at any time;
    (5)   the investment policy and the delegation arrangement are reviewed at least once a **year**;
    (6)   all payments due to the financial expert are on a scale or at a level which is agreed in advance and are notified promptly to the Trustees on receipt; and
    (7)   the financial expert must not do anything outside the powers of the Trustees.

4.14 To arrange for investments or other property of the Charity to be held in the name of a **nominee company** acting under the control of the Trustees or of a financial expert acting under their instructions, and to pay any reasonable fee required.

4.15 To deposit documents and physical assets with any company registered or having a place of business in England and Wales as **custodian,** and to pay any reasonable fee required.

4.16 To insure the property of the Charity against any foreseeable risk and take out other insurance policies to protect the Charity when required.

4.17 To pay for **indemnity insurance** for the Trustees.

4.18 Subject to clause 5, to employ paid or unpaid agents, staff or advisers.

4.19 To enter into contracts to provide services to or on behalf of other bodies.

4.20 To establish or acquire subsidiary companies to assist or act as agents for the Charity.

4.21 To pay the costs of forming the Charity.

4.22 To do anything else within the law which promotes or helps to promote the Objects.

5.   BENEFITS TO MEMBERS AND TRUSTEES

5.1   The property and funds of the Charity must be used only for promoting the Objects and do not belong to the **members** but:
       (1)   members who are not Trustees may be employed by or enter into contracts with the Charity and receive reasonable payment for goods or services supplied;
       (2)   members (including Trustees) may be paid interest at a reasonable rate on money lent to the Charity;
       (3)   members (including Trustees) may be paid a reasonable rent or hiring fee for property or equipment let or hired to the Charity; and
       (4)   [individual] members [who are not Trustees but] [(including Trustees)] who are also **beneficiaries** may receive charitable benefits in that capacity.

5.2   A Trustee must not receive any payment of money or other **material benefit** (whether directly or indirectly) from the Charity except:
       (1)   as mentioned in clauses 4.17 (indemnity insurance), 5.1(2) (interest), 5.1(3) (rent) [, 5.1(4) (charitable benefits)] [or 5.3 (contractual payments)];
       (2)   reimbursement of reasonable out-of-pocket expenses (including hotel and travel costs) actually incurred in the administration of the Charity;
       (3)   an indemnity in respect of any liabilities properly incurred in running the Charity (including the costs of a successful defence to criminal proceedings);
       (4)   payment to any company in which a Trustee has no more than a 1 per cent shareholding; and
       (5)   in exceptional cases, other payments or benefits (but only with the **written** approval of the **Commission** in advance).

5.3   A Trustee may not be an employee of the Charity[, but a Trustee or a **connected person** may enter into a contract with the Charity to supply goods or services in return for a payment or other material benefit if:

(1)   the goods or services are actually required by the Charity;

(2)   the nature and level of the benefit is no more than reasonable in relation to the value of the goods or services and is set at a meeting of the Trustees in accordance with the procedure in clause 5.4; and

(3)   no more than *[number or proportion up to one half]* of the Trustees are interested in such a contract in any **financial year]**.

5.4   Whenever a Trustee has a personal interest in a matter to be discussed at a meeting of the Trustees or a committee, he or she must:

(1)   declare an interest before the meeting or at the meeting before discussion begins on the matter;

(2)   be absent from the meeting for that item unless expressly invited to remain in order to provide information;

(3)   not be counted in the quorum for that part of the meeting; and

(4)   be absent during the vote and have no vote on the matter.

5.5   This clause may not be amended without the written consent of the Commission in advance.

6.   LIMITED LIABILITY

The liability of members is limited.

7.   GUARANTEE

Every member promises, if the Charity is dissolved while he, she or it remains a member or within 12 months afterwards, to pay up to [£10] towards the costs of dissolution and the liabilities incurred by the Charity while he or she was a member.

8.   DISSOLUTION

8.1   If the Charity is dissolved, the assets (if any) remaining after provision has been made for all its liabilities must be applied in one or more of the following ways:

(1)   by transfer to one or more other bodies established for exclusively charitable purposes within, the same as or similar to the Objects;

(2)   directly for the Objects or for charitable purposes which are within or similar to the Objects;

(3)   in such other manner consistent with charitable status as the Commission approve in writing in advance.

8.2 A final report and statement of account must be sent to the Commission.

9.   INTERPRETATION

9.1 Words and expressions defined in the **Articles** have the same meanings in the **Memorandum.**

9.2 References to an Act of Parliament are references to that Act as amended or re-enacted from time to time and to any subordinate legislation made under it.
We wish to be formed into a company under this Memorandum of Association:

NAMES AND ADDRESSES OF SUBSCRIBERS	SIGNATURES OF SUBSCRIBERS
[list the full name and residential address of each of the subscribers]	*[signature of each of the subscribers]*

Date _____   *[date]*

Witness to the above signatures

_____

_____

_____

_____   _____

[name, address and occupation of witness]   *[signature of witness]*

_____

COMPANIES ACTS 1985 AND 1989
COMPANY LIMITED BY GUARANTEE

ARTICLES OF ASSOCIATION OF

_____ *[name]*

1. MEMBERSHIP

1.1 The Charity must maintain a register of **members**.

1.2 **Membership** of the Charity is open to any individual [or organisation] interested in promoting the **Objects** who:
   (1) applies to the Charity in the form required by the **Trustees**;
   (2) is approved by the Trustees; and
   (3) signs the register of members or consents **in writing** to become a member [either personally or (in the case of an organisation) through an **authorised representative**].

1.3 The Trustees may establish different classes of membership (including **informal membership**), prescribe their respective privileges and duties and set the amounts of any subscriptions.

1.4 Membership is terminated if the member concerned:
   (1) gives **written** notice of resignation to the Charity;
   (2) dies [or (in the case of an organisation) ceases to exist];
   (3) is more than six **months** in arrear in paying the relevant subscription, if any (but in such a case the member may be reinstated on payment of the amount due); or
   (4) is removed from membership by resolution of the Trustees on the ground that in their reasonable opinion the member's continued membership is harmful to the Charity. The Trustees may only pass such a resolution after notifying the member in writing and considering the matter in the light of any written representations which the member concerned puts forward within 14 **clear days** after receiving notice.

1.5 Membership of the Charity is not transferable.

2. GENERAL MEETINGS

2.1 Members are entitled to attend general meetings [either] personally [or (in the case of a member organisation) by an authorised representative] [or by proxy. Proxy forms must be delivered to the **Secretary** at least 24 hours before the meeting.] General meetings are called on at least 21 clear days' written notice specifying the business to be discussed.

2.2   There is a quorum at a general meeting if the number of members [or authorised representatives] [personally] present [in person or by proxy] is at least *[number]* or *[percentage]* of the members if greater).

2.3   The **Chairman** or (if the Chairman is unable or unwilling to do so) some other member elected by those present presides at a general meeting.

2.4   Except where otherwise provided by [the **Articles** or] the **Companies Act**, every issue is decided by a majority of the votes cast.

2.5   Except for the chairman of the meeting, who has a [second or] casting vote, every member present in person [or through an authorised representative] [or by proxy] has one vote on each issue.

2.6   A written resolution signed by all those entitled to vote at a general meeting is as valid as a resolution actually passed at a general meeting. For this purpose the written resolution may be set out in more than one document and will be treated as passed on the date of the last signature.

2.7   Except at first, The Charity must hold an **AGM** in every year. The first AGM must be held within 18 months after the Charity's incorporation.

2.8   At an AGM the members:
      (1)   receive the accounts of the Charity for the previous **financial year**;
      (2)   receive the Trustees' report on the Charity's activities since the previous AGM;
      (3)   accept the retirement of those Trustees who wish to retire or who are retiring by rotation;
      (4)   elect Trustees to fill the vacancies arising;
      (5)   appoint auditors for the Charity;
      (6)   may confer on any individual (with his or her consent) the honorary title of Patron, President or Vice-President of the Charity; and
      (7)   may discuss and determine any issues of policy or deal with any other business put before them by the Trustees.

2.9   Any general meeting which is not an AGM is an **EGM**.

2.10 An EGM may be called at any time by the Trustees and must be called within 28 clear days on a written request from at least *[number]* members.

3.   THE TRUSTEES

3.1   The Trustees as **charity trustees** have control of the Charity and its property and funds.

3.2   The Trustees when complete consist of at least [three] and not more than *[number]* individuals, all of whom must be members [aged under [75] years at the date of appointment] [and *any special qualifications*].

3.3   The subscribers to the **Memorandum** are the first Trustees.

3.4   Every Trustee [after appointment or reappointment] must sign a declaration of willingness to act as a charity trustee of the Charity before he or she may vote at any meeting of the Trustees.

3.5   One third (or the number nearest one third) of the Trustees must retire at each AGM, those longest in office retiring first and the choice between any of equal service being made by drawing lots.

3.6   A retiring Trustee who remains qualified may be reappointed [for a maximum of *[number]* consecutive terms of office].

3.7   A Trustee's term of office automatically terminates if he or she:
   (1)   is disqualified under the Charities Act from acting as a charity trustee;
   (2)   is incapable, whether mentally or physically, of managing his or her own affairs;
   (3)   is absent [without notice] from *[number]* consecutive meetings of the Trustees [and is asked by a majority of the other Trustees to resign];
   (4)   ceases to be a member [(but such a person may be reinstated by resolution passed by all the other Trustees on resuming membership of the Charity before the next AGM)];
   (5)   resigns by written notice to the Trustees (but only if at least two Trustees will remain in office);
   (6)   [is removed by resolution of the members present and voting at a general meeting after the meeting has invited the views of the Trustee concerned and considered the matter in the light of any such views;]
   (7)   [reaches the age of [75]; or
   (8)   [ceases to *have the required qualifications*].

3.8   The Trustees may at any time co-opt any individual who is qualified to be appointed as a Trustee to fill a vacancy in their number or as an additional Trustee, but a co-opted Trustee holds office only until the next AGM.

3.9 A technical defect in the appointment of a Trustee of which the Trustees are unaware at the time does not invalidate decisions taken at a meeting.

4. TRUSTEES' PROCEEDINGS

4.1 The Trustees must hold at least *[number]* meetings each year.

4.2 A quorum at a meeting of the Trustees is *[number]* Trustees.

4.3 [A meeting of the Trustees may be held either in person or by suitable electronic means agreed by the Trustees in which all participants may communicate with all the other participants.]

4.4 The Chairman or (if the Chairman is unable or unwilling to do so) some other Trustee chosen by the Trustees present presides at each meeting.

4.5 Every issue may be determined by a simple majority of the votes cast at a meeting, but a written resolution signed by all the Trustees is as valid as a resolution passed at a meeting. For this purpose the resolution may be contained in more than one document and will be treated as passed on the date of the last signature.

4.6 Except for the chairman of the meeting, who has a [second or] casting vote, every Trustee has one vote on each issue.

4.7 A procedural defect of which the Trustees are unaware at the time does not invalidate decisions taken at a meeting.

5. TRUSTEES' POWERS
   The Trustees have the following powers in the administration of the Charity:

5.1 To appoint (and remove) any member (who may be a Trustee) to act as Secretary in accordance with the Companies Act.

5.2 To appoint a Chairman, Treasurer and other honorary officers from among their number.

5.3 To delegate any of their functions to committees consisting of two or more individuals appointed by them. At least [two members] of every committee must be Trustees and all proceedings of committees must be reported promptly to the Trustees.

5.4 To make standing orders consistent with the Memorandum, the Articles and the Companies Act to govern proceedings at general meetings [and to prescribe a form of proxy].

5.5 To make rules consistent with the Memorandum, the Articles and the Companies Act to govern their proceedings and proceedings of committees.

5.6 To make regulations consistent with the Memorandum, the Articles and the Companies Act to govern the administration of the Charity and the use of its seal (if any).

5.7 To establish procedures to assist the resolution of disputes or differences within the Charity.

5.8 To exercise any powers of the Charity which are not reserved to a general meeting.

6. RECORDS AND ACCOUNTS

6.1 The Trustees must comply with the requirements of the Companies Act and of the Charities Act as to keeping financial records, the audit of accounts and the preparation and transmission to the Registrar of Companies and the **Commission** of:
   (1) annual returns;
   (2) annual reports; and
   (3) annual statements of account.

6.2 The Trustees must keep proper records of:
   (1) all proceedings at general meetings;
   (2) all proceedings at meetings of the Trustees;
   (3) all reports of committees; and
   (4) all professional advice obtained.

6.3 Accounting records relating to the Charity must be made available for inspection by any Trustee at any time during normal office hours and may be made available for inspection by members who are not Trustees if the Trustees so decide.

6.4 A copy of the Charity's latest available statement of account must be supplied on request to any Trustee or member. A copy must also be supplied, within two months, to any other person who makes a written request and pays the Charity's reasonable costs.

7. NOTICES

7.1 Notices under the Articles may be sent by hand, by post [or by suitable electronic means] or (where applicable to members generally) may be published in any suitable journal or [national] newspaper [circulating in area of benefit] or any journal distributed by the Charity.

7.2   The only address at which a member is entitled to receive notices
       sent by post is an address [in the U.K.] shown in the register of
       members.

7.3   Any notice given in accordance with these Articles is to be treated
       for all purposes as having been received:
       (1)   24 hours after being [sent by electronic means or] delivered by
              hand to the relevant address;
       (2)   two clear days after being sent by first class post to that
              address;
       (3)   three clear days after being sent by second class or overseas
              post to that address;
       (4)   on the date of publication of a newspaper containing the
              notice;
       (5)   on being handed to the member [(or, in the case of a member
              organisation, its authorised representative)] personally; or, if
              earlier,
       (6)   as soon as the member acknowledges actual receipt.

7.4   A technical defect in the giving of notice of which the Trustees are
       unaware at the time does not invalidate decisions taken at a meeting.

8.   DISSOLUTION
       The provisions of the Memorandum relating to dissolution of the
       Charity take effect as though repeated here.

9.   INTERPRETATION
              In the Memorandum and in the Articles, unless the context
              indicates another meaning:

'AGM' means an annual general meeting of the Charity;
['area of benefit' means *[geographical area]*;]
'the Articles' means the Charity's articles of association;
['authorised representative' means an individual who is authorised by a
       member organisation to act on its behalf at meetings of the Charity
       and whose name is given to the Secretary;]
['beneficiaries'] means *[qualifications of beneficiaries]*;]
['Chairman'] means the chairman of the Trustees;
'the Charity' means the company governed by the Articles;
'the Charities Act' means the Charities Act 1993;
'charity trustee' has the meaning prescribed by section 97(1) of the
       Charities Act;
'clear day' means 24 hours from midnight following the relevant event;
'the Commission' means the Charity Commissioners for England and
       Wales;
'the Companies Act' means the Companies Act 1985;
'connected person' means any spouse, partner, parent, child, brother,
       sister, grandparent or grandchild of a Trustee, any **firm** of which a
       Trustee is a member or employee, and any company of which a

Trustee is a director, employee or shareholder having a beneficial interest in more than 1 per cent of the share capital;

'custodian' means a person or body who undertakes safe custody of assets or of documents or records relating to them;

'EGM' means an extraordinary general meeting of the Charity;

'financial expert' means an individual, company or firm who is authorised to give investment advice under the Financial Services and Markets Act 2000;

'financial year' means the Charity's financial year;

'firm' includes a limited liability partnership;

'indemnity insurance' means insurance against personal liability incurred by any Trustee for an act or omission which is or is alleged to be a breach of trust or breach of duty, unless the Trustee concerned knew that, or was reckless whether, the act or omission was a breach of trust or breach of duty;

'informal membership' refers to a supporter who may be called a 'member' but is not a company member of the Charity.

'material benefit' means a benefit which may not be financial but has a monetary value;

'member' and 'membership' refer to company membership of the Charity;

'Memorandum' means the Charity's Memorandum of Association;

'month' means calendar month;

'nominee company' means a corporate body registered or having an established place of business in England and Wales;

'the Objects' means the Objects of the Charity as defined in clause 3 of the Memorandum;

'Secretary' means the company secretary of the Charity;

'taxable trading' means carrying on a trade or business for the principal purpose of raising funds and not for the purpose of actually carrying out the Objects, the profits of which are subject to corporation tax;

'Trustee' means a director of the Charity and 'Trustees' means the directors.

'written' or 'in writing' refers to a legible document on paper [not] including a fax message;

'year' means calendar year.

9.2 Expressions defined in the Companies Act have the same meaning.

9.3 References to an Act of Parliament are to that Act as amended or re-enacted from time to time and to any subordinate legislation made under it.

[list the full name and residential   *[signature of each of the subscribers]*
address of each of the subscribers]

Date _____   *[date]*

Witness to the above signatures

_____

_____

_____

_____

_____

A3 Charity Law Association: Model Constitution for a Charitable Unincorporated Association (2nd Edition)

1. NAME
    The name of the **Charity** is *[NAME]*.

2. OBJECTS
    The **Objects** are *[OBJECTS]*.

3. POWERS
    The Charity has the following powers, which may be exercised only in promoting the Objects:

3.1 To promote or carry out research.

3.2 To provide advice.

3.3 To publish or distribute information.

3.4 To co-operate with other bodies.

3.5 To support, administer or set up other charities.

3.6 To raise funds (but not by means of **taxable trading**).

3.7 To borrow money and give security for loans (but only in accordance with the restrictions imposed by the **Charities Act**).

3.8 To acquire or hire property of any kind.

3.9 To let or dispose of property of any kind (but only in accordance with the restrictions imposed by the Charities Act).

3.10 To make grants or loans of money and to give guarantees.

3.11 To set aside funds for special purposes or as reserves against future expenditure.

3.12 [To deposit or invest in funds in any manner (but to invest only after obtaining such advice from a **financial expert** as the **Trustees** consider necessary and having regard to the suitability of investments and the need for diversification).]

3.13 [To delegate the management of investments to a financial expert, but only on terms that:
    (1) the investment policy is recorded **in writing** for the financial expert by the Trustees;
    (2) every transaction is reported promptly to the Trustees;

    (3)   the performance of the investments is reviewed regularly with the Trustees;

    (4)   the Trustees are entitled to cancel the delegation arrangement at any time;

    (5)   the investment policy and the delegation arrangement are reviewed at least once a **year**;

    (6)   all payments due to the financial expert are on a scale or at a level which is agreed in advance and are reported promptly to the Trustees on receipt;

    (7)   the financial expert must not do anything outside the powers of the Trustees.]

3.14 To insure the property of the Charity against any foreseeable risk and take out other insurance policies to protect the Charity when required.

3.15 To pay for **indemnity insurance** for the Trustees.

3.16 Subject to sub-clause 9.3, to employ paid or unpaid agents, staff or advisers.

3.17 To enter into contracts to provide services to or on behalf of other bodies.

3.18 To establish or acquire subsidiary companies to assist or act as agents for the Charity.

3.19 To pay the costs of forming the Charity.

3.20 To do anything else within the law which promotes or helps to promote the Objects.

4.   MEMBERSHIP

4.1   **Membership** is open to any individual [or organisation] interested in promoting the Objects.

4.2   The Trustees may establish different classes of membership, prescribe their respective privileges and duties and set the amounts of any subscriptions.

4.3   The Trustees must keep a register of **members**.

4.4   A member whose subscription is six months in arrears ceases to be a member but may be reinstated on payment of the amount due.

4.5   A member may resign by **written** notice to the Charity.

4.6 The Trustees may by resolution terminate the membership of any member on the ground that in their reasonable opinion the member's continued membership would be harmful to the Charity. The Trustees may only pass such a resolution after notifying the member in writing and considering the matter in the light of any written representations which the member puts forward within 14 **clear days** after receiving notice.

4.7 Membership of the Charity is not transferable.

5.   GENERAL MEETINGS

5.1 Members are entitled to attend general meetings of the Charity [either] in person [or (in the case of a member organisation) through an **authorised representative**]. General meetings are called on at least [21] clear days' written notice to the members specifying the business to be transacted.

5.2 There is a quorum at a general meeting if the number of members [or authorised representatives] personally present is at least *[number]*, or *[percentage]* of the members if greater).

5.4 The **Chairman** or (if the Chairman is unable or unwilling to do so) some other member elected by those present presides at a general meeting.

5.5 Except where otherwise provided by this Constitution, every issue at a general meeting is determined by a simple majority of votes cast by the members present in person [or (in the case of a member organisation) through an authorised representative].

5.6 Except for the chairman of the meeting, who has a [second or] casting vote, every member present in person [or (in the case of a member organisation) through an authorised representative] is entitled to one vote on every issue.

5.7 Except at first, an **AGM** must be held in every year. The first AGM may be held at any time within 18 months after the formation of the Charity.

5.8 At an AGM the members:
   (1)   receive the accounts of the Charity for the previous **financial year**;
   (2)   receive the report of the Trustees on the Charity's activities since the previous AGM;
   (3)   accept the retirement of those **elected Trustees** who wish to retire or are retiring by rotation;
   (4)   elect elected Trustees to fill the vacancies arising;

(5)   elect from among the members a Chairman to hold office from the end of the AGM until the end of the next AGM;

(6)   appoint an auditor or **independent examiner** for the Charity where required;

(7)   may confer on any individual (with his or her consent) the honorary title of Patron, President or Vice-President of the Charity; and

(8)   discuss and determine any issues of policy or deal with any other business put before them by the Trustees.

5.9   Any general meeting which is not an AGM is an **EGM**.

5.10 An EGM may be called at any time by the Trustees and must be called within 14 clear days after a written request to the Trustees from at least *[number]* members.

6.   THE TRUSTEES

6.1   The Trustees as **charity trustees** have control of the Charity and its property and funds.

6.2   The Trustees when complete consists of at least three and not more than *[number]* individuals, all of whom must be members or [authorised representatives] [aged under 75 years at the date of the appointment] [and *add any special qualifications.*]

6.3   The Trustees consist of:

(1)   the Chairman;

(2)   *[number]* elected Trustees. One third (or the number nearest one third) of the elected Trustees must retire at each AGM, those longest in office retiring first and the choice between any of equal service being made by drawing lots;

(3)   [*[number]* **nominated Trustees**, appointed by *[name[s] of appointing body/ies]*, to hold office until the end of the AGM *[number]* years later;]

(4)   [up to *[number]* **co-opted Trustees,** appointed by resolution of the Trustees to hold office until the end of the next AGM.]

6.4   A retiring Trustee who remains qualified may be re-appointed [for a maximum of [three] consecutive terms of office].

6.5   Every Trustee after appointment or reappointment must sign a declaration of willingness to act as a charity trustee of the Charity before he or she may vote at any meeting of the Trustees.

6.6   A Trustee's term of office automatically terminates if he or she:

(1)   is disqualified under the Charities Act from acting as a charity trustee;

(2)   is incapable, whether mentally or physically, of managing his or her own affairs;

(3)   is absent [without notice] from *[number]* consecutive meetings of the Trustees [and is asked by a majority of the other Trustees to resign];

(4)   ceases to be a member of the Charity [(but such a person may be reinstated by resolution of all the other members of the Trustees on resuming membership of the Charity before the next AGM);]

(5)   resigns by written notice to the Trustees (but only if at least two Trustees members will remain in office);

(6)   [is removed by a resolution passed by all the other Trustees after they have invited the views of the Trustee concerned and considered the matter in the light of any such views;]

(7)   [reaches the age of 75; or]

(8)   [ceases to *have the required qualifications.*]

6.7   A retiring Trustee is entitled [on written request] to an indemnity from the continuing Trustees at the expense of the Charity in respect of any liabilities properly incurred while he or she held office.

6.8   A technical defect in the appointment of a Trustee of which the Trustees are unaware at the time does not invalidate decisions taken at a meeting.

7.   TRUSTEES' PROCEEDINGS

7.1   The Trustees must hold at least *[number]* meetings each year.

7.2   A quorum at a meeting of the Trustees is *[number]* Trustees.

7.3   [A meeting of the Trustees may be held either in person or by suitable electronic means agreed by the Trustees in which all participants may communicate with all other participants.]

7.4   The Chairman or (if the Chairman is unable or unwilling to do so) some other member of the Trustees chosen by the Trustees present presides at each meeting of the Trustees.

7.5   Every issue may be determined by a simple majority of the votes cast at a meeting of the Trustees but a resolution which is in writing and signed by all the Trustees is as valid as a resolution passed at a meeting and for this purpose the resolution may be contained in more than one document and will be treated as passed on the date of the last signature.

7.6   Except for the chairman of the meeting, who has a [second or] casting vote, every Trustee has one vote on each issue.

7.7   [A procedural defect of which the Trustees are unaware at the time does not invalidate decisions taken at a meeting of the Trustees.]

8.   TRUSTEES' POWERS
The Trustees have the following powers in the administration of the Charity:

8.1   To appoint a Treasurer and other honorary officers from among their number.

8.2   To delegate any of their functions to committees consisting of two or more individuals appointed by them (but at least [two] members of every committee must be Trustees and all proceedings of committees must be reported promptly to the Trustees).

8.3   To make standing orders consistent with this Constitution to govern proceedings at general meetings.

8.4   To make rules consistent with this Constitution to govern their proceedings and proceedings of committees.

8.5   To make regulations consistent with this Constitution to govern the administration of the Charity (including the operation of bank accounts and the commitment of funds).

8.6   To resolve, or establish procedures to assist the resolution of, disputes within the Charity.

8.7   To exercise any powers of the Charity which are not reserved to a general meeting.

9.   BENEFITS TO MEMBERS AND TRUSTEES

9.1   The property and funds of the Charity must be used only for promoting the Objects and do not belong to the members or the Trustees.

9.2   No Trustee may receive any payment of money or other **material benefit** (whether direct or indirect) from the Charity except:
      (1)   under sub-clauses 3.15 (indemnity insurance) and 9.3 (contractual payments);
      (2)   reimbursement of reasonable out-of-pocket expenses (including hotel and travel costs) actually incurred in the administration of the Charity;
      (3)   interest at a reasonable rate on money lent to the Charity;
      (4)   a reasonable rent or hiring fee for property let or hired to the Charity;

(5) an indemnity in respect of any liabilities properly incurred in running the Charity (including the costs of a successful defence to criminal proceedings);

(6) payment to a company in which the Trustee has no more than a 1 per cent shareholding;

(7) [charitable benefits in his or her capacity as a **beneficiary**;] and

(8) in exceptional cases, other payments or material benefits (but only with the prior written approval of the Commission).

9.3 A Trustee may not be an employee of the Charity, but a Trustee or **connected person** may enter into a contract with the Charity to supply goods or services in return for a payment or other material benefit, but only if:

(1) the goods or services are actually required by the Charity;

(2) the nature and level of the benefit is no more than reasonable in relation to the value of the goods or services and is set at a meeting of the Trustees in accordance with the procedure in sub-clause 9.4; and

(3) not more than [*[number or proportion up to one half]*] of the Trustees are interested in any such contract in any one financial year.

9.4 Whenever a Trustee has a personal interest in a matter to be discussed at a meeting of the Trustees or a committee, he or she must:

(1) declare an interest before the meeting or at the meeting before discussion begins on the matter;

(2) be absent from that part of the meeting unless expressly invited to remain in order to provide information;

(3) not be counted in the quorum for that part of the meeting;

(4) be absent during the vote and have no vote on the matter.

10. PROPERTY AND FUNDS

10.1 Funds which are not required for immediate use (including those which will be required for use at a future date) must be placed on deposit or invested in accordance with clause 3.12 until needed.

10.2 Investments and other property of the Charity may be held:

(1) in the names of the Trustees for the time being (or in the corporate name of the Trustees if incorporated under the Charities Act);

(2) in the name of a **nominee company** acting under the control of the Trustees or of a financial expert acting on their instructions;

(3) in the name of at least two and up to four holding trustees for the Charity who may be appointed (and removed) by resolution of the Trustees;

(4) in the name of a **trust corporation** as a holding trustee for the Charity, which must be appointed (and may be removed) by deed executed by the Trustees;

(5) in the case of land, by the Official Custodian for Charities under an order of the Commission or the Court.

10.3 Documents and physical assets may be deposited with any company registered or having a place of business in England and Wales as **custodian**.

10.4 Any nominee company acting under sub-clause 10.2(2), any trust corporation appointed under sub-clause 10.2(4) and any custodian appointed under sub-clause 10.3 may be paid reasonable fees.

11. RECORDS AND ACCOUNTS

11.1 The Trustees must comply with the requirements of the Charities Act as to the keeping of financial records, the audit or independent examination of accounts and the preparation and transmission to the Commission of:

(1) annual returns;

(2) annual reports; and

(3) annual statements of account.

11.2 The Trustees must keep proper records of:

(1) all proceedings at general meetings;

(2) all proceedings at meetings of Trustees;

(3) all reports of committees; and

(4) all professional advice obtained.

11.3 Accounting records relating to the Charity must be made available for inspection by any Trustee at any time during normal office hours and may be made available for inspection by members if the Trustees so decide.

11.4 A copy of the Charity's latest available statement of account must be supplied on request to any Trustee or member. A copy must also be supplied, within two **months**, to any other person who makes a written request and pays the Charity's reasonable costs.

12. NOTICES

12.1 Notices under this Constitution may be sent by hand, by post [or by suitable electronic means] or (where applicable to members generally) may be published in any suitable journal or [national] newspaper [circulating in area of benefit] or any journal distributed by the Charity.

12.2 The address at which a member is entitled to receive notices is the address noted in the register of members (or, if none, the last known address).

12.3 Any notice given in accordance with this Constitution is to be treated for all purposes as having been received:
  (1) 24 hours after being [sent by electronic means or] delivered by hand to the relevant address;
  (2) two clear days after being sent by first class post to that address;
  (3) three clear days after being sent by second class post or overseas post to that address;
  (4) on the date of publication of a journal or newspaper containing the notice;
  (5) on being handed to the member [or its authorised representative] personally or, if earlier,
  (6) as soon as the member acknowledges actual receipt.

12.4 A technical defect in the giving of notice of which the members or the Trustees are unaware at the time does not invalidate decisions taken at a meeting.

13. AMENDMENTS
This Constitution may be amended at a general meeting by a [two-thirds] majority of the votes cast, but:

13.1 The members must be given [21] clear days' notice of the proposed amendments.

13.2 No amendment is valid if it would make a **fundamental change** to the Objects or to this clause or destroy the charitable status of the Charity.

13.3 Clause 9 may not be amended without the prior written consent of the Commission.

14. [INCORPORATION

14.1 The Trustees may apply to the Commission under the Charities Act for a certificate of incorporation relating to the Trustees but only after consulting the members at a general meeting.

14.2 The members at a general meeting may authorise the Trustees to transfer the assets and liabilities of the Charity to a limited company established for exclusively charitable purposes within, the same as or similar to the Objects and of which the members of the Charity will be entitled to be members.

14.3 On a transfer under clause 14.2 the Trustees must ensure that all necessary steps are taken as to:
   (1)   the transfer of land and other property;
   (2)   the novation of contracts of employment and transfer of pension rights; and
   (3)   the trusteeship of any property held for special purposes.]

15. DISSOLUTION

15.1 If at any time members at a general meeting decide to dissolve the Charity, the Trustees will remain in office as charity trustees and will be responsible for the orderly winding up of the Charity's affairs.

15.2 After making provision for all outstanding liabilities of the Charity, the Trustees must apply the remaining property and funds in one or more of the following ways:
   (1)   by transfer to one or more other bodies established for exclusively charitable purposes within, the same as or similar to the Objects;
   (2)   directly for the Objects or charitable purposes within or similar to the Objects; or
   (3)   in such other manner consistent with charitable status as the Commission approve in writing in advance.

15.3 A final report and statement of account relating to the Charity must be sent to the Commission.

16. INTERPRETATION
     In this Constitution:

16.1 'AGM' means an annual general meeting of the Charity;

   ['area of benefit' means *[geographical area]*]
   ['authorised representative' means an individual who is authorised by a member organisation to act on its behalf at meetings of the Charity;]
   ['beneficiary' means *[definition]*;]
   ['the Chairman'] means the chairman of the Charity elected at the AGM;
   'the Charity' means the charity comprised in this Constitution;
   'charity trustees' has the meaning prescribed by section 97(1) of the Charities Act;
   'the Charities Act' means the Charities Act 1993;
   'clear day' means 24 hours from midnight following the relevant event;
   'the Commission' means the Charity Commissioners for England and Wales;
   'connected person' means any spouse, partner, parent, child, brother, sister, grandparent or grandchild of a Trustee, any **firm** of which a Trustee is a member or employee or a company of which a Trustee is

a director, employee or shareholder being beneficially entitled to more than 1 per cent of the share capital;

['co-opted Trustees' means those Trustees who are appointed by the Trustees in accordance with clause 6.3(4);]

'custodian' has the meaning prescribed by section 17(2) of the Trustee Act 2000;

'EGM' means a general meeting of the members of the Charity which is not an AGM;

'elected Trustees' means those Trustees who are elected at the AGM;

['financial expert' means an individual, company or firm who is authorised to give investment advice under the Financial Services and Markets Act 2000;]

'financial year' means the Charity's financial year;

'firm' includes a limited liability partnership;

'fundamental change' means such a change as would not have been within the reasonable contemplation of a person making a donation to the Charity;

'holding trustee' means an individual or corporate body responsible for holding the title to property but not authorised to make any decisions relating to its use, investment or disposal;

'indemnity insurance' means insurance against personal liability incurred by any Trustee for an act or omission which is or is alleged to be a breach of trust or breach of duty, unless the Trustee concerned knew that, or was reckless whether, the act or omission was a breach of trust or breach of duty;

'independent examiner' has the meaning prescribed by section 43(3)(a) of the Charities Act;

'material benefit' means a benefit which may not be financial but has a monetary value;

'member' and 'membership' refer to membership of the Charity;

'months' means calendar months;

['nominated Trustees' means those Trustees appointed by outside persons or bodies in accordance with clause 6.3(3);]

'the Objects' means the charitable objects of the Charity set out in clause 2;

'taxable trading' means carrying on a trade or business on a continuing basis for the principal purpose of raising funds and not for the purpose of actually carrying out the Objects;

'trust corporation' has the meaning prescribed by section 205(1)(cxxviii) of the Law of Property Act 1925 (but does not include the Public Trustee);

'the Trustee' means a member of the governing body of the Charity and 'Trustees' the members of the governing body;

'written' or 'in writing' refers to a legible document on paper including a fax message;

'year' means calendar year.

16.2 References to an Act of Parliament are references to the Act as amended or re-enacted from time to time and to any subordinate legislation made under it.

ADOPTED AT A MEETING HELD AT *[PLACE]* ON *[DATE]*

SIGNED

Name.......................................

Signature...

[name and signature of chairman of meeting]

WITNESSED

Name.......................................

Address ....

....

Occupation...

Signature...

[name, address, occupation and signature of witness]

A4   Model Fundraising Agreement for Fundraising Consultant/Professional Fundraiser

Date:

Between:

The Client (1) and the Provider (2) each of whose details are set out in Schedule 1.

BACKGROUND:

(A)   The Client wishes to raise funds for its public benefit objects and specifically the purposes stated in the Specification.

(B)   The Provider has expertise in the provision of fundraising services.

Terms and conditions:

1.   INTERPRETATION

Definitions and interpretation provisions set out in Schedule 7 apply.

2.   SERVICE DELIVERY

2.1   The Provider shall in the capacity specified in Schedule 1 provide the Fundraising Services in the applicable Area (if any) for the Contract Period, in accordance with the Specification and the Standards.

2.2   The Provider shall, for the Contract Period, maintain a Provider Contact approved by the Client (such approval not to be unreasonably withheld).

3.   STANDARDS

3.1   The Provider shall provide the Fundraising Services to the Client with reasonable care, skill and diligence, in accordance with:

3.1.1   all applicable legal requirements;

3.1.2   the Institute of Fundraising Code of Practice, 'Best Practice for Fundraising Contracts' and any other code of practice applicable to the Provider, and/or the Fundraising Services and/or this Agreement and/or (as notified in writing to the Provider) the Client;

3.1.3   the elements in the Specification prescribing service standards;

3.1.4   obligations of the Client under any grant, contract, or statutory duty, or otherwise as notified in writing by the Client to the Provider;

3.1.5   further reasonable Client instructions within the scope of the Specification.

3.2   The Provider shall in providing the Fundraising Services act at all times in the manner which:

3.2.1   promotes the public benefit purposes of the Client;

3.2.2   in the reasonable opinion of the Client does not and is not likely to damage its good name, image, reputation, or intellectual property rights;

3.2.3   is not misleading and does not impose upon or create for the Client any liability (except any expressly provided for under this Agreement).

3.3   If there is any inconsistency between the principal terms and conditions of this Agreement and/or the Specification and/or the Standards, or between any of the Standards (subject to contrary agreement) the more demanding requirement shall apply.

3.4   Without prejudice to Clause 3.1 the Provider shall ensure that:

3.4.1   it has adequate resources to provide the Fundraising Services properly and efficiently throughout the Contract Period;

3.4.2   Provider Personnel are fully and properly trained and supervised in accordance with and fully comply with all specified criteria and requirements in the Standards;

3.4.3   Provider sub–contractors are reasonably selected and supervised and comply with the terms and conditions of this Agreement.

3.5   The Provider shall (without prejudice to Clause 3.1), comply with any agreed minimum requirements and use its reasonable endeavours to meet any agreed performance targets.

3.6   If the Provider is a Professional Fundraiser, the Professional Fundraiser statutory statement agreed in Schedule 3 shall be made in relation to every representation in relation to this Agreement that funds are being raised for charitable purposes.

4.   CLIENT'S OBLIGATIONS

The Client shall:

4.1   provide all co-operation, information and support reasonably requested by the Provider in relation to its provision of the Services;

4.2   provide access to all operational and financial information reasonably requested by the Provider to enable to it perform its obligations under this Agreement;

4.3 ensure all decisions of the Client in relation to this Agreement are made with proper authority emanating from its Board of Trustees (or governing committee) and that they are integrated with the Client's other operational, fundraising and promotional activities;

4.4 maintain a Client Contact for the Contract Period;

4.5 perform any specific Client obligations set out in the Specification.

5. PAYMENTS TO THE PROVIDER

5.1 In return for the Fundraising Services the Client shall make payments of fees (including applicable expenses) to the Provider, on the payment terms set out in Schedule 4.

5.2 All payments under this Agreement are exclusive of applicable VAT unless otherwise stated.

5.3 All expenses which the Provider is entitled to claim under this Agreement in addition to, or as part of, payments for the services, shall be payable only against receipts, or other written evidence that they were properly incurred, as reasonably required by the Client.

6. LATE PAYMENT INTEREST

Each party shall be entitled to charge interest at 4% above the base rate for the time being of the Client's principal bank, calculated on a daily basis on the balance of any overdue payment due to it from the other party (before and after any judgment).

7. LIAISON, REPORTING AND REVIEW

7.1 The parties shall ensure that their authorised representatives and in particular the Primary Contacts meet as often as is necessary during the Contract Period for the proper and efficient delivery of the Fundraising Services and at least as often as is specified in Schedule 5.

7.2 The Provider shall, in addition to oral reporting in and outside meetings, provide written reports containing reasonable detail to the Client during and at the end of the Contract Period, as specified in Schedule 5, in respect of its performance of the Fundraising Services with reference to Key Performance Indicators.

7.3 The parties shall undertake formal reviews of this Agreement in accordance with any review timetable specified in Schedule 5 and at least a reasonable time prior to any prospective renewal date.

8.   RECORD KEEPING, RIGHTS OF INSPECTION

8.1   Each party shall apply proper financial and management systems and properly maintain and update records (respectively, in accordance with any requirements specified in Schedule 5), for the Contract Period and maintain them for at least two years after termination or expiry of this Agreement.

8.2   Each party shall on reasonable notice and at reasonable times and otherwise in accordance with the other's reasonable instructions, permit any authorised representative of the other, and in the case of the Provider, any funder or regulator of the Client requiring such access under its arrangements with the Client, to inspect and take copies of any of the records and the Provider shall procure for the Client and such funders and regulators the same rights in respect of all Provider Sub-contractors.

9.   CLIENT INTELLECTUAL PROPERTY RIGHTS

The Client licenses the Provider, as non-exclusive licensee for the Contract Period, in delivering the Fundraising Services, in accordance with this Agreement only, to use Client intellectual property rights in accordance with necessarily implied or express provisions of this Agreement (including the Client's reasonable instructions) and nothing in relation to this Agreement shall otherwise imply any transfer or further licensing of any such rights.

10.   COPYRIGHT AND DATABASE RIGHTS

10.1   The Provider assigns copyright and database rights to the Client in all Client specific materials (in any medium) generated under this Agreement.

10.2   Such assignment does not extend to rights in material developed by the Provider independently from this Agreement, or generic materials produced under this Agreement, except as incorporated into Client specific materials.

10.3   The Provider grants the Client a non-exclusive, perpetual, non-transferable, royalty-free licence to use such incorporated generic material to the extent it is so incorporated.

11.   CONFIDENTIALITY AND PUBLICITY

11.1   Both parties shall keep in confidence any information of a confidential nature obtained under this Agreement, or relating to this Agreement and shall not use or divulge it to any person without the written consent of the other party.

11.2 The preceding clause does not apply to information:

    11.2.1 in the public domain (otherwise than by breach of this Agreement);

    11.2.2 in the lawful possession of the receiving party prior to the date of this Agreement (other than through liaison between the parties prior to and in anticipation of this Agreement);

    11.2.3 obtained from a third party free to divulge it;

    11.2.4 required to be disclosed by a Court or other competent authority;

    11.2.5 properly disclosed on a confidential basis to personnel, sub-contractors or professional advisers of the respective parties, for the purposes of this Agreement.

11.3 No public announcement or other publicity concerning this Agreement shall, unless required by law or competent authority, be made, or issued, by cither party, without the prior written consent of the other.

12. DATA CAPTURE AND PROTECTION

12.1 The Provider shall capture such Data under this Agreement and in such form as may be prescribed in the Specification.

12.2 All Data supplied by the Client to the Provider, or captured by the Provider, or any Provider Sub-contractor shall be used by the Provider and (as the Provider shall procure) any Provider Sub-contractor, only for the purposes of and in accordance with the provisions of this Agreement.

12.3 The Provider shall, on termination or expiry of this Agreement, as soon as is reasonably practicable, return or provide (as applicable) all copies of such Data to the Client or destroy all such copies in accordance with the Client's reasonable instructions.

12.4 Each party shall ensure that all its respective legal obligations concerning data protection are complied with in respect of all Data.

13. INDEMNITY

13.1 The Provider shall indemnify the Client in respect of any liability to any third party arising as a result of any acts or omissions of Provider Personnel, or Provider Sub-contractors, employed or engaged by the Provider in relation to this Agreement.

13.2 The Client shall ensure that the Provider is reasonably consulted and informed by the Client in relation to any claims made, or proceedings initiated, by any third party which are relevant to Clause 13.1 and in particular that the Provider has a reasonable opportunity to comment on the terms of any proposed payment or settlement of any such claim or proceedings.

14. INSURANCE

14.1 The Provider shall have in place and maintain for and in relation to the Contract Period appropriate insurance against all risks normally covered by a comprehensive policy of insurance in respect of the provision of services in the nature of the Fundraising Services, including adequate public liability insurance.

14.2 The Provider shall, on request, provide to the Client a copy of the insurance policy or policies required under Clause 14.1 with reasonable evidence of payment of the respective current premium(s).

15. LIMITATION OF LIABILITY

The appropriateness of any limitation of liability under this Agreement has been specifically explained by the party seeking such limitation, specifically agreed and is set out in Schedule 6.

16. TERMINATION

16.1 Any right of termination of this Agreement by written notice is specified in Schedule 1.

16.2 Either party may terminate this Agreement forthwith by written notice if the other party:
16.2.1 has committed a fundamental breach of this Agreement;
16.2.2 is in breach of the Agreement and has failed to remedy such breach within 14 days of receipt of a written notice from the notifying party requiring the breach to be remedied;
16.2.3 repeats any breach in respect of which a remedy notice was issued;
16.2.4 commits or suffers any Insolvency Event.

16.3 The Client shall be entitled to terminate this Agreement forthwith by written notice if:
16.3.1 Any Key Individual specified in the Specification ceases to be personally available to deliver the Services for a material period and is not replaced to the satisfaction of the Client;
16.3.2 the Provider becomes subject to the Control of any party which does not Control it at the Agreement Date.

17. CONSEQUENCES OF TERMINATION

17.1 In the event of any termination of this Agreement (provided termination is not by reason of the Client's default) the Client shall be entitled, at its option, to assume direct responsibility for the relevant fundraising activities and/or to appoint any third party or parties to promote and continue such activities and the Provider shall provide reasonable co-operation to ensure, as far as possible, continuity of such activities.

17.2 Any right to terminate and the Client's right under Clause 17.1 are without prejudice to any other rights in respect of any relevant breach and to rights which accrued prior to termination.

17.3 Any provision of this Agreement which expressly or by necessary implication is intended to have effect after expiry or termination of this Agreement shall continue to have such effect for the intended further period.

18. AMENDMENT

The Agreement may be amended only in writing signed by or on behalf of each party (subject to any rights of either party in writing and on reasonable notice reasonably to update or vary, payment provisions, the Specification, or any other provision of this Agreement, as specified in Schedules 4 or 5).

19. FORCE MAJEURE

19.1 Neither party shall be liable for any delay in performing any of its obligations under this Agreement if such delay is caused by circumstances beyond its reasonable control, (subject to giving the other party full particulars of the circumstances and using all reasonable endeavours to resume performance as soon as possible). Such circumstances shall not include strikes or industrial disputes (except where affecting similar businesses in similar circumstances), failures by sub-contractors (except where due to strikes or industrial disputes affecting similar businesses in similar circumstances) or shortages of labour.

19.2 A party exposed to force majeure delay under Clause 19.1 shall be entitled to terminate this Agreement on written notice.

20. NON-WAIVER

No forbearance or delay by either party in enforcing provisions of this Agreement shall prejudice or restrict the rights of that party, nor shall any waiver of rights in respect of any breach of this Agreement operate as a waiver of any rights in respect of any other breach.

21. ASSIGNMENT AND SUB-CONTRACTING

21.1 Neither party may assign the benefit of this Agreement without the written consent of the other.

21.2 The Provider may only sub-contract performance of its obligations under this Agreement, as specified in the Specification, or as agreed in writing by the Client.

22. DISPUTE RESOLUTION

22.1 Any dispute arising in connection with this Agreement shall be notified in writing by one party to the other and shall first be addressed by direct personal liaison between the respective Primary Contacts.

22.2 If any dispute has not been resolved under clause 22.1 within 10 Working Days of such notification, the matter shall (if applicable) be referred to be resolved by direct liaison between more senior individuals nominated by each party.

22.3 If any dispute has not been resolved by such senior officers within a further 10 Working Days the matter may be referred at the option of either party, within a further 5 Working Days, to mediation in accordance with the Model Mediation Procedure for the time being of the Centre for Dispute Resolution (Registered Company Number: 2422813; Registered Charity Number 1060369; www.cedr.co.uk) and where any such reference is made neither party shall commence legal proceedings in respect of the relevant matter until such procedure is complete.

23. NOTICES

23.1 Any notice from either party to the other under this Agreement may be personally delivered, or sent by recorded delivery to the address of the other party as set out in the heading to this Agreement, or as otherwise notified in writing, or by transmission, with due transmission receipt, to a fax number or e-mail address notified in writing for the purpose.

23.2 Any personally delivered, faxed or e-mailed notice shall be deemed received on the day it was delivered or sent if it was delivered or sent on a Working Day before 4.30pm and otherwise on the next Working Day.

24. ENTIRE AGREEMENT

The Agreement (incorporating its Schedules) is the exclusive statement of the agreement between the parties in relation to the Fundraising Services. It supersedes all previous communications, representations, arrangements and agreements between the parties relating to the Fundraising Services.

25. THIRD PARTIES RIGHTS

This Agreement does not and is not intended to provide any third party with any rights under the Contracts (Rights of Third Parties) Act 1999 or otherwise.

26. LAW

This Agreement is governed by and shall be construed in accordance with the law of England and Wales, unless otherwise specified in Schedule 2.

27. SPECIAL TERMS AND CONDITIONS

The above terms and conditions apply subject to any special terms and conditions set out in Schedule 6.

In Witness the parties have below executed this Agreement with effect from the date in the heading

Signed:

On behalf of the Client

Name:

Position:

Signed:

On behalf of the Provider

Name:

Position:

Schedule 1

Particular contract details

1. CLIENT DETAILS

Name:

Legal Status:

Registered/Principal Office:

Registered Company Number:

Registered Charity Number:

2. PROVIDER DETAILS

Name:

Legal Status:

Registered/Principal Office:

Registered Company Number:

3. PROVIDER FUNDRAISER STATUS IN RELATION TO THIS AGREEMENT

[Professional Fundraiser/Consultant/both]

4. Fundraising Objectives

4.1 Objectives

4.2 Means of achieving them

5. Contract Period

From:

To:

6. TERMINATION ON NOTICE PROVISION

This Agreement may be terminated by [one or either party] giving [_____] [weeks/months] written notice to the other [up to [_____]]

7. AREA

The Provider is appointed to provide the Fundraising Services in the following geographical area:

[_____].

8. GOVERNING LAW

[N.B. any drafting changes required by Scottish/Northern Irish law]

Schedule 2

Specification

1. [Description of Fundraising Services and delivery timescales]

2. [Provisions relating to the transfer of funds to the Client]

3. [Resources to be applied by Provider in delivering the Fundraising Services]
   3.1 Key personnel
   3.2 Money
   3.3 Materials
   3.4 Equipment
   3.5 Other]

4. [Resources to be applied by Client in supporting delivery of the Fundraising Services
   4.1 Key personnel
   4.2 Office space
   4.3 Money
   4.4 Information
   4.5 Materials
   4.6 Equipment
   4.7 Other]

5. [Outputs
   – Performance Requirements;
   – Targets to be pursued with reasonable endeavours]

6. [Key Performance Indicators]

7. [Milestones].

Schedule 3

Professional fundraiser statutory statement (if applicable)

Example: [Provider] will receive a fee of £x for services provided in relation to this [fundraising campaign].

X, a registered charity, and Y, a registered charity, will each receive 50% of the net proceeds.

[*NB.   The agreed statement must reflect the actual arrangements*].

Schedule 4

Payments to provider

1.   [Fee payment schedule]

2.   [Expenses schedule]

3.   [Payment terms]

4.   [Price variation mechanism (if applicable)]

Schedule 5

Contract management provisions

1.   [Provider Contact details]

2.   [Client Contact details]

3.   [Liaison meeting regime]

4.   [Reporting regime]

5.   [Review/renewal process]

Schedule 6

Special terms and conditions

1.   [Any agreed limitation of liability – see Clause 15]

2.   [Any agreed amendment procedure – see Clause 18]

3.   [Any variation to the principal terms and conditions – see Clause 27]

4.   [Any other special terms and conditions]

Schedule 7

Interpretation

1.   In the Agreement the following definitions apply:

'Agreement Date'   the date of this Agreement;

'Area'	as specified in Schedule 2;
'Client Contact'	the principal individual contact of the Client for the purposes of this Agreement;
'Contract Period'	as specified in Schedule 2;
'Control'	ultimate control over more than 50% of the votes governing decisions in a relevant organisation;
'Data'	all regulated data captured, controlled or processed in relation to this Agreement;
'Fundraising Services'	as outlined in Schedule 1 and detailed in the Specification;
'Insolvency Event'	the calling of any creditors meeting; the appointment of any receiver, administrator, or administrative receiver over all or any part of assets or undertaking; the presentation of a winding-up or bankruptcy petition; the convening of a meeting to pass a winding up resolution; entering into liquidation; a bankruptcy petition issued in respect of any director, owner or key individual; the suspension or cessation of business; any threat to suspend or cease business;
'IOF Code'	the codes of practice for the time being of the Institute of Fundraising (Registered Charity Number: 1079573; www.institute-of-fundraising.org.uk);
'Key Performance Indicators'	as specified in the Specification;
'Primary Contacts'	the Client Contact and Provider Contact;
'Provider Contact'	the principal individual contact of the Provider for the purposes of this Agreement;
'Provider Personnel'	every individual employed or engaged by the Provider in delivering any part of the Fundraising Services, whether as agents, consultants, employees, independent contractors, volunteers or otherwise;
'Provider Sub-contractors'	every corporate person or other organisation providing services to the Provider in relation to this Agreement, including every individual employed or engaged by such sub-contractor in delivering any part such services, whether as agents, consultants, employees, independent contractors, volunteers or otherwise;

'Specification'   the methodology, content and details of the
                                   Fundraising Services as specified in Schedule 2
                                   (as amended from time to time by agreement
                                   between the parties);

'Standards'   as specified in Clause 3;

'Working Day'   9.30am to 5.00pm Monday to Friday excluding
                                   official bank holidays in England and Wales.

2.   In this Agreement (subject to manifest contrary intention):
      2.1   the singular includes the plural and vice versa;
      2.2   references to clauses, sub-clauses and schedules are to clauses,
            sub-clauses and schedules to this Agreement;
      2.3   headings to clauses are for reference only and not
            interpretation;
      2.4   references to statutory provisions respectively include any
            provision which amends, replaces or supplements them;
      2.5   every indicative list, or use of the words 'including' or 'in
            particular', or any cognate, or similar words apply without
            limitation and without prejudice to the generality.

NOTE
   1.   This model contract was produced by Bates Wells & Braithwaite for the Best
         Practice for Fundraising Contracts section of the Institute of Fundraising's
         Codes of Fundraising Practice for all Voluntary and Community Organisations.
         Guidance on the use of this contract is to be found in the code (see
         www.institute-of-fundraising.org.uk).

A5   Model Gift Aid Declaration

Name of
Charity   _____

Details of donor

Title   Fore-   Sur-
                name(s)   name

Ad-
dress   _____

                                    Post
                                    Code

_____   _____

I want the charity to treat

*   the enclosed donation of £   _____ as a Gift Aid
         donation

*   the donation(s) of £   _____   which I made
         on _____ / _____ / _____ as (a) Gift Aid
         donation(s)

*   all donations I make from the date of this declaration until I notify
         you otherwise as Gift Aid donations

*   all donations I have made for the six years prior to this year (but no
         earlier than 6 April 2000), **and** all donations I make from the date of
         this declaration until I notify you otherwise, as Gift Aid donations.

delete as appropriate

**You must pay an amount of Income Tax and/or Capital Gains Tax at least
equal to the tax that the charity reclaims on your donations in the
appropriate tax year (currently 28p for each £1 you give).**

Date: _____ / _____ / _____

Notes

1.   You can cancel this declaration at any time by notifying the charity.

2.   If in the future your circumstances change and you no longer pay
      tax on your income and capital gains equal to the tax that the charity
      reclaims, you can cancel your declaration.

3.   If you pay tax at the higher rate you can claim further tax relief in
      your Self Assessment tax return.

4.   If you are unsure whether your donations qualify for Gift Aid tax relief, ask the charity. Or, refer to help sheet IR65 on the HMRC web site.

5.   Please notify the charity if you change your name or address.

A6 Model Sponsorship and Gift Aid Declaration Form

CHARITY X: SPONSORSHIP AND GIFT AID DECLARATION FORM

We, who have given our names and addresses below, and who have ticked the box entitled '(√) Gift Aid?', want the above charity to reclaim tax on the donation detailed below, given on the date shown. We understand that each of us must pay income tax or capital gains tax equal to the tax reclaimed by the charity on the donation.

Details of Sponsors

Full name	Home address	Post code	Amount pledged	Amount given	Date given (dd/mm/yy)	Gift Aid? (√)

Total donations: £

To be completed by the charity:

Date moneys received

Total amount of Gift Aid donations £ _____ x22/78 = £ _____ tax reclaimable

A7   Model Charity Repayment Claim Form

Inland Revenue
IR Charities

Charity Repayment Claim

The box below is for Inland Revenue use only | Please complete if the Reference, Charity name and Address boxes are blank.

Date claim received / /	**Reference**
Claim sub no.	**Charity name**
Arith. check Initials _____ Date / /	**Address**
Authorised Initials _____ Date / /	
√ *if appropriate* Notification ☐ Advice ☐	

Please

- **Read R68(Notes)** before completing this claim.
- Use *CAPITAL LETTERS* when filling out this form and √ boxes as appropriate.
- Tell us immediately if the charity's name changes or if you are a new signatory. Don't wait until you claim repayment as any change may cause delay.
- Make a copy of the claim or schedules if you need to before sending them.
- Don't send correspondence unless it relates to the claim.
- When you have finished fold this form in half and use the return envelope provided.
- Make sure that the address, to which you are returning the form, is clearly visible in the envelope window.

Part 1   Amount of repayment claim

In respect of each source of income below:

- complete the appropriate schedule, and
- enter the tax/relief claimed.

Tax/relief claimed

1   Other income received under deduction of tax.
Enter the total amount of tax deducted - Schedule R68(F).

1 £ [   ]

2   New Gift Aid
Enter the total amount claimed from Schedule R68 (New Gift Aid)

2 £ [   ]

3   Transitional relief on distributions paid on or after 6 April 1999.
Enter the total relief claimed - Schedule R68(TCTR).

3 £ [   ]

add boxes 1,2, and 3

4   Total tax/relief claimed.

4 £ [   ]

5   **Sponsored Events**
Has the charity included donations received from Sponsored fundraising event(s) in this claim? For example, Sponsored Walks, Marathons, Cycle Rides.

√ *as appropriate*
Yes ☐   No ☐

R68(2000)   BS 4/04

Part 2 Charity details

1 Is the charity's name as shown overleaf?

Yes ☐   No ☐

If 'No', please enter the correct name of the charity below and send a copy of the document confirming the change of name.

2 Is the charity a company for tax purposes?
(See note 5)

Yes ☐   No ☐

If 'Yes' please enter the date the accounts period ends *(See note 6)*

Day ☐   Month ☐

All repayments are now dealt with in our Bootle office. Please send all completed forms to the address printed opposite. If you have any questions about the repayment process please call **08453 02 02 03**.

Inland Revenue Charities
Repayments (Code 361A)
St John's House
Merton Road
Bootle, Merseyside
L69 9BB

Part 3 Repayment details

1 Period to which the claim relates.

From   /   /

To   /   /

Building society reference number

Account number

sort code   —   —

2 Where is the repayment to be sent?
Tick one of the following boxes.

- direct to your bank or building society ☐
- to a nominee ☐
- by cheque to the address shown overleaf ☐
- by cheque to a different address ☐

3 Fill in this section if the repayment is to be sent to your, or your nominee's, bank building society account.

Name of bank or building society

Name of account for use BACS
(first 28 characters including spaces)

4 Authorisation - fill in this section if the repayment is to be sent to a nominee or to a different address.

Nominee's name and reference *(if appropriate)*

Nominee's address

Name and address to which cheque should be sent

Name and address for acknowledgement to be sent

Signature of an authorised officer of the charity

Part 4 Declaration

An authorised official of the charity must complete and sign the Declaration

1 Title ☐   Full name ☐

2 Your official position, for example, Treasurer, Secretary, Trustee.

3 Phone number at which we may contact you if we have a question about this claim.

I claim the sum of £ ☐ as shown in box 4 overleaf.

I declare to the best of my knowledge and belief:
- the information given on this form is correct and complete and
- the charity is exempt from tax under Sections 505, 507 or 508 ICTA 1988 in respect of the income shown on this form.

I understand that false statements can lead to prosecution.

Signed ☐   Date   /   /

A8   Model Charity Official Authorisation Form

Charity Official Authorisation form

Inland **Revenue**
Financial Intermediaries and
Claims Office

Charity name

FICO Charity reference   Charity Commission or Scottish Charities Index reference (if applicable)

Charity address

Post code

Please complete Part A below to let me have details of the official who will sign your repayment claims. We will repay claims only if they are signed by this authorised official. If you wish to change the authorised official, you must inform us in writing, providing all the details requested in Part A.

Having completed Part A please also complete Part B before returning this form.

We will send any queries about claims to the authorised official at the address shown on the claim form (R68).

PART A

Details of the Authorised Official:

Full name   Office hours contact telephone number (where possible)

Home address   National Insurance Number

Signature of Authorised Official

Post code

PART B

Signature   **Full name in CAPITALS**

Capacity in which signed   **Date**

APPENDIX B

TRUSTEES ANNUAL REPORTING

B1   Companies Act 2006 – Checklist of Actions to Take

Trading subsidiaries and charitable companies

The Companies Act is the longest Act ever considered by the UK Parliament and the breadth and variety of material covered by the Act is very significant. The new law applies throughout the United Kingdom, so companies in Northern Ireland, as well as Scotland and England and Wales, need to consider its implications.

There are also many sets of supplementary regulations. The transitional rules and procedures in these are particularly important. They produce considerably different effects for pre-existing companies compared to companies that are newly incorporated after each set of new rules come into force. Each set of regulations should therefore be considered very carefully in relation to individual companies.

Charities would be well advised to work through this checklist to ensure they are dealing properly with the legal and practical implications of this "monster" of an Act! Consider the actions in relation to trading subsidiaries as well as the charity (if the latter is in the legal form of a company limited by guarantee).

*   **Healthcheck** the memorandum and articles for out of date, inconsistent and unhelpful provisions, see http://www.jordans.co.uk/ jordans3.nsf/Main/Healthcheck

*   Arrange necessary alterations and updating of the memorandum and articles in consequence.

*   Arrange suitable training for board members, officers and senior staff.

*   Acquire up to date reference works and books.

*   Determine whether you have a constitutional obligation to hold an AGM and consider whether there will be practical difficulties if you abandon doing so.

*   If you are continuing to hold an AGM, review and adjust all documents and procedures, to meet the many new and different Companies Act rules regarding general meetings and members' rights.

*   Review and update all other precedents and documents.

*   Review all literature, communications, websites and web pages, standard footers on e mails, notices on premises etc and adjust / add wording to comply with the enhanced public declarations of status and details that are required.

*   Revitalise your approach to the contents, layout and presentation of the trustees' annual report, in preparation for the further legal requirements that are looming.

*   Trustees should arrange a general review of their charity's trading subsidiaries and the relationship of those to the charity.

Jordans can assist with all of the above matters, contact Cecile Gillard e-mail cecile_gillard@jordans.co.uk or call 0117 9181319.

B2   Trustees' Annual Report – Key Issues

GENERAL

The Statement of Recommended Practice – accounting by charities ("SORP") requires a trustees' annual report to be prepared to accompany the annual accounts of a charity. SORP sets out the major areas this report must deal with and gives details as to what information must be included for each area. These notes provide comments in relation to:

*   The main areas that must be covered in the annual trustees' report of a charity of medium to large size (ie one that is NOT entitled to claim small charity exemptions such as preparing its annual accounts on a "receipts and payments" basis).

*   The wider key issues for trustees in relation to their annual report.

Whilst there are relaxations for smaller charities, so that they are only obliged to give more limited information, their trustees should consider best practice and may wish to follow the pattern required of charities in general.

CHARITABLE COMPANIES LIMITED BY GUARANTEE

A charity in the legal form of a private company limited by guarantee is, of course, subject to company law obligations in relation to annual accounts and reports, as modified for companies that are charities. Essentially, the company law obligations relating to a directors' report to accompany the annual accounts can be combined with the charity law and SORP obligations, so that one composite report meets both sets of legal requirements (company law and charity law). That single report can them be used to meet both sets of filing requirements – the charity law obligation to file the annual accounts and trustees' report with the relevant charity regulator(s) (the Charity Commission and/or Office of the Scottish Charity Regulator) and the company law obligation to file with the Registrar of Companies.

MAIN SORP REQUIREMENTS

Reference and administrative material about the charity, its trustees and advisors

This section must give the charity's full **legal name** (as on the relevant charity register) plus any other name by which it is known (eg an operational name) and the **charity registration number**(s). If the charity is registered in both England and Wales and Scotland the two numbers will be different (the Scottish charity number will be prefixed "SC"). If the charity is in the legal form of a company, its **company number** must also be stated.

The address of the principal office must be given and, for a charitable company, the address of its registered office.

The names of all trustees must be stated, this should include all who served for any part of the year being reported on. If trustees have joined the board after that year but before the approval of the report, their names should also be given.

The name of the Chief Executive Officer and the names of any staff to whom the trustees have delegated day to day management must be given (is senior management staff).

Names and addresses of all relevant professional advisers must be stated (eg solicitors, bankers, auditors or reporting accountants/independent examiners, investment advisers).

Structure, governance and management

This section must set out the legal form of the charity (unincorporated charitable trust, unincorporated members' association, charitable company limited by guarantee etc); specify the nature of the governing document (eg trust deed or memorandum and articles of association); and set out the methods for appointing trustees.

There should be details of how new trustees are inducted, plus information about the general training and development of trustees.

The organisational structure must be described (eg committees and their roles, in the context of the governance role of the trustee board) and the decision-making processes explained.

If the charity is part of a wider network information about that should be given (eg the Wildlife Trusts partnership).

Details of relationships with related parties must be given. Note that SORP defines "related parties".

There must be a statement about risk management, including the review processes by which risks are identified and the systems and procedures adopted by the board to manage those risks.

Objectives and activities

This section should make clear the aims and objectives set by the charity, the strategies and activities undertaken to achieve those and set matters in the context of the longer term strategies and objectives that have been set.

The information must include a summary of the charitable purposes (as set out in the governing document); an explanation of the charity's aims, including what changes or differences it seeks to make by its activities; an explanation of the main objectives for the year being reported on and the strategies for achieving the stated objectives, details of significant activities that contribute to obtaining the objectives.

If the charity makes grants as a major activity, the grantmaking policy must be stated.

If there are material social investment programmes and/or material use of volunteers, information must be provided about those areas.

Achievements and performance

This section must give information about the achievements of the charity (and any subsidiaries) during the year being reported on. In particular it should review the charitable activities, explaining performance against objectives, give details of material fundraising activities, again including performance achieved against objectives set and commenting on material expenditure as well as projected future income.

Details of material investments and their performance against the investment objectives should be given.

Any factors outside the charity's control that are relevant to the achievement of its objectives should be commented upon. Those might include relationships with employees, service users, other beneficiaries and funders and the charity's position in the wider community.

Financial review

A review of the charity's financial position is required (and that of any subsidiaries). The principal financial management policies adopted during the year should be stated.

The policy on financial reserves, the level of reserves held and why they are held must be indicated. If material sums have been designated for particular purposes the amounts and reasons must be given, together with intended timing of future expenditure. If there is a deficit or surplus on the target reserves sums this must be indicated, together with the steps being taken to address the difference.

Principal funding sources must be given.

There must be information about how expenditure during the year has supported the charity's key objectives.

If there are material investments, the investment policy and its objectives, including any social, environmental or ethical considerations, should be indicated.

Plans for future periods

The charity's plans for future periods need to be explained, including key aims and objectives and details of activities planned to support those.

Funds held as custodian trustee

If the charity holds any funds in the capacity of "custodian trustee" details must be given.

KEY ISSUES FOR TRUSTEES

In this section the notes highlight some key issues for trustees in relation to their annual report:

Report fully, honestly and accurately Trustees should remember the need for honesty and transparency. All that ought to be included in the report should be. The details should be complete and there should be no attempt to "window dress" or in any way hide information.

Explain and justify! Trustees must be willing to set out what they have done and what they plan to do and why.

Remember the basics An astonishing number of trustees' reports have errors or omissions in the basic factual information, such as names of trustees.

Be honest about financial reserves Having the right financial reserves policy and ensuring the levels of reserves decided upon are achieved, plus regularly reviewing both policy and performance against it are fundamentals of sound financial management. Trustees should include such activities as an inherent part of their management of and stewardship of the charity.

Remember why the charity exists and what the trustees' role is The very nature of a charity is to be an organisation that exists for others. It holds funds and assets for specific charitable purposes to benefit the public. Accountability, in a variety of forms, is an essential part of the legal regime for safeguarding charitable assets and ensuring that the purposes are pursued and that the public benefits from the charity's activities.

Use the report positively and creatively It offers a golden opportunity to demonstrate that your charity is well governed and that its trustees are discharging their responsibilities well; to explain that it delivers real value by way of public benefit; to gain good publicity and avoid adverse criticism; to encourage continuing and further support for the charity and what it does, and, taking the wider view, to help champion the cause of the entire charity sector.

APPENDIX C

OFFICIAL ADDRESSES[1]

Arts Council
14 Great Peter Street, London SW1P 3NQ
Tel 020 7333 0100

The Charity Commissioners
St Alban's House, 57-60 Haymarket, London SW1Y 4QX
Tel 020 7210 4477

Woodfield House, Tangier, Taunton, Somerset TA1 4BL
Tel 01823 345 000

2nd Floor, 20 King's Parade, Queen's Dock, Liverpool L3 4DQ
Tel 0151 703 1500

Church Commissioners
1 Millbank, London SW1P 3JZ
Tel 020 7898 1000

For **Revenue & Customs and DSS enquiries**
contact the local enquiry office.

Department for Children, Schools and Families
Sanctuary Building, Great Smith Street, London SW1P 3BT
Tel 0870 000 2288

Department of Health
Richmond House, 79 Whitehall, London SW1A 2NS
Tel 020 7210 4850

Department for Culture, Media and Sport
3rd Floor, 2-4 Cockspur Street, London SW1Y 5DH
Tel 020 7211 6000

Gaming Board for Great Britain
Berkshire House, 168-173 High Holborn, London WC1V 7AA
Tel 020 7306 6200

---

[1]   Reproduced with kind permission of the Charity Law Association.

Housing Corporation
149 Tottenham Court Road, London W1T 7BN
Tel 020 7387 9466

Inland Revenue (Claims Branch)
Trusts and Charities, St John's House, Merton Road, Bootle L69 9BB
Tel 0151 472 6000 (covenants) or 0151 933 2819 (other)

Inland Revenue Claims (Scotland)
Trinity Park House, South Trinity Road, Edinburgh EH3 3SD
Tel 0131 551 8127

Big Lottery Fund
1 Plough Place, London EC4A 1DE
Tel 08454 102030

National Heritage Memorial Fund
7 Holbein Place, London SW1W 8NR
Tel 0207 591 6042

National Lottery Charities Board (head office)
7th Floor, Vincent House, 30 Orange Street, London WC2H 7HH
Tel 020 7839 5371

Registrar of Companies
Companies House, Crown Way, Cardiff CF4 3UZ
Tel 01222 380 801

Registrar of Companies (Scotland)
Companies House, 37 Castle Terrace, Edinburgh EH2 2EB
Tel 0131 5355 5800

Registrar of Friendly Societies
15 Marlborough Street, London W1V 1AF
Tel 020 7437 9992

Office of the Scottish Charity Regulator
2nd Floor, Quadrant House, 9, Riverside Drive, DundeeDD1 4NY
Tel 01382 346890

Scottish Office, Education Department
Victoria Quay, Edinburgh EH6 6QQ
Tel 0131 556 8400

Sports England
3rd Floor Victoria House, Bloomsbury Square, London WC1B 4SE
Tel 020 7273 1551

Treasury Solicitor's Department
One Kemble Street, London WC2B 4TS
Tel 020 7210 3000

APPENDIX D

HELPFUL ORGANISATIONS[1]

Action with Communities in Rural England (ACRE)
Strand Road, Cirencester GL7 6JR
Tel 01285 653 477

Almshouse Association
Billingbear Lodge, Carters Hill, Wokingham, Berkshire RG40 5RU
Tel 01344 52922

Association of Charitable Foundations (ACF) (Grant-makers only)
High Holborn House, 52-54 High Holborn, London WC1V 6RL
Tel 0171 404 1338

Association of Chief Executives of National Voluntary Organisations (ACENVO)
31-33 College Road, Harrow HA1 1EJ
Tel 0181 424 2334

Centre for Dispute Resolution (CEDR) Charities Unit
7 St Katharine's Way, London E1 9LB
Tel 0171 481 4441

Charities Aid Foundation (Gifts to charity, publications etc)
114 Southampton Row, London WC1B 5AA
Tel 0171 831 7798

Charity Appointments (Recruitment consultants)
3 Spital Yard, London E1 6AQ
Tel 0171 247 4502

Charity Finance Directors Group
Tanners Lane, Ilford, Essex
Tel 0181 503 9217

Charity Forum (Training, PR, fundraising, management)
Stovolds, 191 The Street, West Horsley, Surrey KT24 6HR
Tel 01483 281 766

---

[1]   Reproduced with kind permission of the Charity Law Association.

Charity Law Association
Bouverie House, 154 Fleet Street, London EC4A 2DQ
Tel 0171 353 0299

Charity People (Recruitment consultants)
Station House, 150 Waterloo Road, London SE1 8SB
Tel 0171 620 0062

Charity Recruitment (Recruitment consultants)
40 Rosebery Avenue, London EC1R 4RN
Tel 0171 833 0770

Community Matters (Community associations etc)
8-9 Upper Street, London N1 0PQ
Tel 0171 226 0189

Directory of Social Change (Training, publications)
24 Stephenson Way, London NW1 2DG
Tel 0171 209 4949

Dundee University (Charity Law Research Unit)
Department of Law, Dundee DD1 4HN
Tel 01382 223 181 Fax 01382 226 905

Institute of Charity Fundraising Managers (ICFM)
208 Market Towers, 1 Nine Elms Lane, London SW8 5NQ
Tel 0171 627 3436/3508

Institute of Chartered Secretaries and Administrators (ICSA) (Charities Group – training, publications)
16 Park Crescent, London W1N 4AH
Tel 0171 580 4741

Joseph Rowntree Foundation (Publications, research)
The Homestead, 40 Water End, York YO3 6LP
Tel 01904 629 241

London School of Economics (Centre for Voluntary Organisations)
Houghton Street, London WC2A 2AE
Tel 0171 405 7686

Liverpool University (Charity Law Unit)
Faculty of Law, PO Box 147, Liverpool L69 3BX
Tel 0151 794 3088 Fax 0151 794 2829

National Council for Voluntary Organisations (NCVO) (Training, publications, advice)
Regent's Wharf, 8 All Saints Street, London N1 9RL
Tel 0171 713 6161

National Federation of Housing Associations
175 Gray's Inn Road, London WC1X 8UE
Tel 0171 278 6571

Scottish Charity Finance Directors' Group
72 Charlotte Street, Glasgow G1 5DW
Tel 0141 303 3131

Scottish Council for Voluntary Organisations (SCVO)
18-19 Claremont Crescent, Edinburgh EH7 4QD
Tel 0131 556 3882

South Bank University Business School (Course in charity finance)
103 Borough Road, London SE1 0AA
Tel 0171 928 8989

Trustee Register (Finding trustees)
23 Peascod Street, Windsor, Berkshire SL4 1DE
Tel 01753 868 277

NB This list is not exhaustive; apologies to those inadvertently omitted.

APPENDIX E

FURTHER READING

JOURNALS

Most 'umbrella' and specialist bodies publish both an annual report and their own journal or newsletter, eg NCVO News, Trust and Foundation News (ACF), the Almshouse Gazette, Strategy Matters (the Charities Strategic Management Forum).

General charity journals include Third Sector, Charity, and Local Charity.

More specialist journals: for example NGO Finance, Charity Law and Practice Review, Charity Finance Yearbook.

CONFERENCES AND TRAINING

Charity Secretarial Administration Seminar – www.jordanstraining.co uk

Charity Accounting and Reporting – www.jordanstraining.co.uk

Charity Trustee Training Toolkit. Available online and on CD – www.jordanstraining.co.uk

Charities and Voluntary Sector Department, Jordans Limited, 21 St Thomas Street, Bristol BS1 6JS

TEXTBOOKS

Moule and Alexander: Charity Governance (Jordans, 2007)

Lloyd: Charities – The New Law 2006 (Jordans, 2007)

Lloyd: Charity Trading and the Law (Jordans, 2008)

Lloyd: Social Enterprise (Jordans, 2008)

Bawtree and Kirkland: Charity Administration Handbook (Tottel, 2008)

Morris: Schools, an Education in Charity Law (Dartmouth, 1996)

Randall and Williams: Charity and Taxation (ICSA, 2008)

Tudor: Charities (Sweet & Maxwell, 2003)

Vincent and Francis: Charity Accounting and Taxation (Tottel, 2004)

Gillard, Van Duzer and Leighton: Jordans Company Secretarial Precedents (Jordans, 2008)

Van Duzer: Companies Act 2006: A Guide for Private Companies (Jordans, 2007)

ENCYCLOPAEDIAS AND LOOSELEAF WORKS

Halsbury's Laws of England: (Charities title)

Butterworth's Encyclopaedia of Forms and Precedents: (Charities and Charitable Giving title)

Jordans Charities Administration Service

Charities: the Law and Practice (Thomson Sweet & Maxwell)

ICSA Charities Administration

Croner's Charities Manual

Tolley's Charities Manual

The Complete Book of Model Fund-raising Letters (Prentice Hall)

USEFUL WEBSITES AND INFORMATION

NCVO – www.ncvo.vol.org.uk

ACEVO – www.acevo.org.uk

Charity Trustee Network – www.trusteenet.org.uk

Charity Directors Finance Group – www.cfdg.org.uk

Institute of Fundraising – www.institute-of-fundraising.org.uk

Institute of Chartered Secretaries and Administrators (Charity Secretaries Group) – www.icsa.org.uk

Fundraising Standards Board – www.frsb.org.uk

Charity Law Association – www.charitylawassociation.org.uk

Charity Commission – www.charitycommisssion.gov.uk

Following a consultation the Charity Commission issued statutory guidance on public benefit in January 2008. This is guidance about public benefit and what charity trustees should consider in order to show that their charity's aims are for the public benefit. A further period of consultation is taking place and final versions are due to be published at the end of the year. Further information can be found at the Charity Commission's website.

INDEX

References are to paragraph numbers.

Academic institutions 4.8.2
  training 4.8.2
Accounting 3.1, 3.2, 3.2.1, 3.2.2, 3.2.3,
  3.2.4, 3.2.5, 3.2.6, 3.3, 3.4, 3.4.1,
  3.4.2, 3.4.3, 3.4.4, 3.4.5, 3.4.6
  audit 3.3
  rates 3.4, 3.4.1
  property used for charitable
    purposes 3.4.2
  tax 3.4, 3.4.1, 3.4.2, 3.4.3, 3.4.4,
    3.4.5, 3.4.6
Accounts 3.2
  annual report 3.2.5
  branches 3.2.6
  formats 3.2.3
  policies 3.2.4
  small charities 3.2.2
  structure 3.2.1
Amalgamation 2.6, 2.6.1, 2.6.1.1,
  2.6.1.2, A1
  transfer of assets 2.6.1
    scheme 2.6.1.2
    statutory power 2.6.1.1
Amendment (constitutional)
  trust deed A1
Annual accounts
  constitutional clauses on
    articles of association A2
    trust deed A1
    unincorporated association A3
Annual report 3.2.5
Applications for assistance 3.8.2, 3.8.3
Articles of association 2.5.1
  changing 2.5.1
  company limited by guarantee A2
Audit 3.3

Branches 3.2.6
  accounts 3.2.6
Buildings 3.7

Capital gains tax 3.4.1
CEDAG 5.5
Certificate of incorporation 3.7.1.1
Charitable purposes 1.1.1, 1.1.3
Charitable status 1.4
  examples 1.4

Charity 1.1, 1.1.1, 1.1.2, 1.1.3, 1.3.5,
  2.1
  constitutional requirements 2.1
  meaning 1.1, 1.1.1, 1.1.2, 1.1.3
    England and Wales 1.1.1, 1.1.3
    Scotland 1.1.2
  reputation 1.3.5
Charity Commission 2.3, 2.3.1, 2.3.2,
  2.3.3, 2.3.4, 2.3.5, 2.3.6, 2.3.7,
  2.7.4, 4.9.6.2
  inquiry 4.9.6.2
  registration 2.3
    excepted charities 2.3.2
    exempt charities 2.3.1
    HMRC 2.3.5
    name of charity 2.3.4
    number 2.3.6
    registration pack 2.3.3
    significance 2.3.7
  winding up 2.7.4
Charity consultants 4.5.4
Charity trustee 1.2, 1.3, 1.3.1, 1.3.2,
  1.3.3, 1.3.4, 1.3.5
  contracts with third parties 1.3.4
  delegation 1.3.3
  duties 1.3.5
  meaning 1.2
  responsibilities 1.3
    conflict 1.3.2
    public trust 1.3.1
Commercial participators 3.11.1
Commission 5.3.4, 5.4.1
  functions 5.4.1
Committee
  unincorporated association A3
Committee of Permanent
  Representatives 5.3.2
Committee of the Regions 5.3.9
Common investment funds 3.6.1
Companies Act 2006 B1
Compensation 4.9.5
Computers
  Equipment 4.6.2
Conflict of duties
  charity trustee 1.3.2

Constitution   2.5, 2.5.1, 2.5.2, 2.5.3,
                          2.5.3.1, 2.5.3.2, 2.5.3.2.1,
                          2.5.3.2.2, 2.5.4, 2.5.5
  changing   2.5, 2.5.1
    alternative procedures   2.5.3,
                   2.5.3.1, 2.5.3.2, 2.5.3.2.1,
                                2.5.3.2.2, 2.5.4
    cy-pres doctrine   2.5.3.2.2
    express power   2.5.2
    new governing instrument   2.5.5
    procedure   2.5.3.2.1
    reviewing aims and
        procedures   2.5.4
    scheme   2.5.3.2
    statutory power   2.5.3, 2.5.3.1
Constitutional requirements   2.1
Consultant
  fundraising
    model form of contract   A4
Continuing education   4.8
Contract culture   4.5.2
Contracts   1.3.4
  third parties   1.3.4
Corporate charity
  guarantee, company limited by   A2
  incorporation procedure   A2
Council of Europe   5.3.11
Council of Ministers   5.3.1
Court of Session   2.7.4
  winding up   2.7.4
Cross-border charitable giving   5.6.2
Cy-pres doctrine   2.8
  changing constitution   2.5.3.2.2
  examples   2.8

Data protection
  fundraiser agreement provisions   A4
Decisions   5.2.4
Declaration of trust   2.2
Directives   5.2.3
Director   4.4.10
  relationship with trustees   4.4.10
  trustee, as   A2
Directorates General   5.3.5
Dissolution   A2
  charitable trust   A1
  unincorporated association   A3

Economic and Social Committee   5.3.8
Emergencies   4.9.1
Employees   1.3.3, 4.4, 4.4.1, 4.4.2, 4.4.3,
                4.4.4, 4.4.5, 4.4.6, 4.4.7, 4.4.8,
                                 4.4.9, 4.8.5
  encouragement or praise when
        deserved   4.4.4
  fairness   4.4.7
  freedom from annoyance   4.4.3
  freedom from insecurity   4.4.2
  health and safety legislation   4.4.9
  interviewing   4.4.1
  opportunities   4.8.5
  pension rights   4.4.8
  policy guidelines   1.3.3

Employees—*continued*
  remuneration   4.4.8
  support for weaknesses   4.4.5
  training   4.4.6
Equipment   4.6, 4.6.1
  computers   4.6.2
Europe   5.1, 5.1.1, 5.5, 5.6.1, 5.6.2
  associations   5.1
  consultation   5.6.1
  cross-border charitable giving   5.6.2
  foundations   5.1
  networks   5.5
  recent developments   5.6.1
  umbrella bodies   5.5
**European Centre for Vocational
    Training**   5.4.6
European Council   5.3.3
European Foundation   5.3.10, 5.4.4
  functions   5.4.4
European Foundation Centre   5.5
European institutions   5.3, 5.4, 5.4.1,
                      5.4.2, 5.4.3, 5.4.4, 5.4.5
  Commission   5.3.4, 5.4.1
  Committee of Permanent
      Representatives   5.3.2
  Council of Europe   5.3.11
  Council of Ministers   5.3.1
  Directorates General   5.3.5
  European Council   5.3.3
  European Foundation   5.3.10, 5.4.4
  European Parliament   5.3.6, 5.3.7,
                         5.3.8, 5.3.9, 5.4.2
  European Social Committee   5.4.3
  interaction   5.4
  non-governmental
      organisations   5.4.5
European law   5.2, 5.2.1, 5.2.2, 5.2.3,
                                5.2.4, 5.2.5
  Decisions   5.2.4
  Directives   5.2.3
  Opinions   5.2.5
  Recommendations   5.2.5
  Regulations   5.2.2
  treaties   5.2.1
European Parliament   5.3.6, 5.4.2
  Committee of the Regions   5.3.9
  committees   5.3.7
  Economic and Social
      Committee   5.3.8
  functions   5.4.2
European programmes   5.4.6
European Social Committee   5.4.3
  functions   5.4.3
European Union   5.1, 5.1.1
  social economy   5.1, 5.1.1
  social tourism   5.1.1
Exclusively charitable purposes   1.1.3
Exempt charities   2.3.1, 2.3.2

Formation of charity   2.1, 2.2
  Act of Parliament   2.1
  charitable incorporated
      association   2.1

Formation of charity—*continued*
choosing legal form 2.2
company limited by guarantee 2.1
declaration of trust 2.1, 2.2
industrial and provident society 2.1
Royal Charter 2.1
unincorporated charitable
association 2.1
will 2.1
Formation of trust
Scotland 2.2
Fundraising 3.9, 3.9.1, 3.9.2, 3.9.3,
3.9.4, 3.9.5, 3.9.5.1, 3.9.5.2,
3.9.6, 3.12.2
agreements 3.9.5
England and Wales 3.9.5.1
Scotland 3.9.5.2
consultant
model agreement A4
managing 3.9.1
methods 3.9.2
model contract A4
offences 3.9.6
records 3.9.4
restrictions on 3.9.3
trading for purpose of 3.12.2
Funds
memorandum of association A2
trust deed provisions A1

General charitable intention 3.10.2.2
Gift Aid
declaration form A5
sponsorship and declaration A7
Gifts 3.10, 3.10.1, 3.10.2, 3.10.2.1,
3.10.2.2, 3.10.2.3, 3.10.3
accepting 3.10
failure of purpose 3.10.2.1, 3.10.2.2,
3.10.2.3
avoiding 3.10.3
general charitable intention 3.10.2.2
identifiable donors 3.10.2.3
refusal to accept 3.10.1
subject to conditions 3.10.2,
3.10.2.1
Grants 3.8, 3.8.1, 3.8.2, 3.8.3
applications for assistance 3.8.2
objective of 3.8.1
policy guidelines 3.8.3

Health and safety legislation 4.4.9
HM Revenue and Customs
registration 2.3.5

Income tax 3.4.1, 3.4.3, 3.4.4, 3.4.5,
3.4.6
Incorporation
forms A2
procedure A2
Insurance 3.5, 3.5.1, 3.5.2, 3.5.3, 3.5.4,
3.5.5, 3.5.6, 3.5.7, 4.9.2
damage 3.5.1

Insurance—*continued*
employer's liability 3.5.3
fidelity 3.5.4
fire 3.5.1
liability 3.5.6
limited liability company 3.5.7
particular risks 3.5.5
public liability 3.5.3
terrorism 3.5.2
theft 3.5.1
vandalism 3.5.2
**International Society for Third
Sector Research** 5.5
Investment 3.6, 3.6.1, 3.6.2, 3.6.2.1,
3.6.2.2, 3.6.3, 3.6.3.1, 3.6.4,
3.6.4.1, 3.6.5
advice on 3.6.3
advisers 3.6.3.1
common investment funds 3.6.1
holding of investments 3.6.4
incorporation 3.6.4.1
land 3.6.5
powers 3.6.2
scheme 3.6.2.2
statutory powers 3.6.2.1
Investments
financial expert, use of (deed
clauses) A1

Land 3.7, 3.7.1, 3.7.1.1, 3.7.1.2, 3.7.2,
3.7.2.1, 3.7.2.2, 3.7.3, 3.7.4
disposal of
Scotland 3.7.4
exchange 3.7.2, 3.7.2.1
formalities 3.7.2.2
holding 3.7.1
certificate of
incorporation 3.7.1.1
land vested in Official
Custodian 3.7.1.2
leasing 3.7.2, 3.7.2.1
formalities 3.7.2.2
mortgage of 3.7.3
sale 3.7.2, 3.7.2.1
formalities 3.7.2.2
Legacies 3.10
accepting 3.10
Limited liability company
insurance 3.5.7
Listed buildings 4.7.3
Lord Advocate 4.9.6.3
powers 4.9.6.3

Management 4.1, 4.5.1, 4.5.2, 4.5.4
charity consultants 4.5.4
coherence 4.5.3
contract culture 4.5.2
planning
time 4.5.1
Mediation 4.9.7

Meetings (members')
constitutional provisions
general meetings (corporate
charity) A2
unincorporated association A3
Meetings (trustees')
trust deed provision A1
Member
constitution provisions
corporate charity A2
unincorporated constitution A3
Memorandum of association 2.5.1
alteration 2.5.1
company limited by guarantee A2
subscribers to A2
Money 3.1, 3.2, 3.2.1, 3.2.2, 3.2.3,
3.2.4, 3.2.5, 3.2.6, 3.3, 3.4, 3.4.1,
3.4.2, 3.4.3, 3.4.4, 3.4.5, 3.4.6
Mortgage
land, of 3.7.3

Name
constitutional provisions A2
unincorporated association A3
Name of charity 2.3.4
National Council for Voluntary
Organisations 5.5
National Lottery 3.9
Negligence 4.9.3
Neighbours 4.7.5
Non-governmental organisations 5.4.5
Notice
unincorporated association
provisions A3

Objects
memorandum of association, in A2
trust deed, in A1
unincorporated association A3
Official Custodian
land vested in 3.7.1.2
Opinions 5.2.5

Patrons 3.11
commercial participators 3.11.1
Pension rights
employees 4.4.8
Planning
time 4.5.1
Powers
memorandum of association, in A2
Premises 4.7, 4.7.1, 4.7.2, 4.7.3, 4.7.4,
4.7.5
appearance 4.7.1
listed buildings 4.7.3
moving 4.7.4
neighbours 4.7.5
regulations 4.7.2

Professional advisers 4.3, 4.3.1, 4.3.1.1,
4.3.1.2, 4.3.2, 4.3.3, 4.3.4, 4.3.5,
4.3.6
barristers 4.3.5
beauty parades 4.3.6
charity consultants 4.3.5
choosing 4.3.1
communication with 4.3.2
effectiveness 4.3.2
fees 4.3.1.1
mistakes to avoid 4.3.4
paralegals 4.3.5
particular specialists 4.3.5
problems with 4.3.3
relationship with trustees 4.3.1.2
solicitors 4.3.5
Professional fundraiser
contract
model form A4
Property 3.1, 3.2, 3.2.1, 3.2.2, 3.2.3,
3.2.4, 3.2.5, 3.2.6, 3.3, 3.4, 3.4.1,
3.4.2, 3.4.3, 3.4.4, 3.4.5, 3.4.6
constitution, clauses in
unincorporated association A3
memorandum of association, in A2
trust deed provisions A1
Public trust 1.3.1
responsibilities of trustees 1.3.1

Rates 3.4, 3.4.1
property used for charitable
purposes 3.4.2
Recommendations 5.2.5
Record keeping 3.3, 3.4, 3.4.1, 3.4.2,
3.4.3, 3.4.4, 3.4.5, 3.4.6
branches 3.2.6
Record-keeping 3.2
formats 3.2.3
policies 3.2.4
small charities 3.2.2
structure 3.2.1
Records
corporate charity A2
trustee A1
unincorporated charity A3
Register of Charities 1.4
Registered office 4.7
Registration 2.3, 2.3.1, 2.3.2, 2.3.3,
2.3.4, 2.3.5, 2.3.6, 2.3.7, 2.4
Charity Commission 2.3
excepted charities 2.3.2
exempt charities 2.3.1
HMRC 2.3.5
name of charity 2.3.4
number 2.3.6
registration pack 2.3.3
significance 2.3.7
information pack A1
Scotland 2.4
Regulations 5.2.2
Remuneration
employees 4.4.8
Reviewing aims and procedures 2.5.4

Running out of money 4.9.6.1

Self-help 4.8.1
Small charities 3.2.2
  accounts 3.2.2
Social economy 5.1, 5.1.1
Social tourism 5.1.1
Sponsors 3.11
  commercial participators 3.11.1
Sponsorship
  gift aid relief
    declaration form A7
Stationery 4.6, 4.6.1
  legal requirements 4.6, 4.6.1
Subscribers
  memorandum of association, to A2

Tax 3.4, 3.4.1, 3.4.2
  gift, relief on A5
  gifts 3.4.5
  HM Revenue and Customs
    guidance 3.4.6
  payments from supporters 3.4.3
  payroll deduction scheme 3.4.4
  repayments
    authorisation form A8
    claim form A7
Technical skills 4.8.3
  training 4.8.3
Tenants 4.9.4
  defaults 4.9.4
Time
  management 4.5.1
Trading 3.12, 3.12.1, 3.12.2
  activities as adjunct to charitable
    purpose 3.12.1
  fundraising, for 3.12.2
Training 4.8, 4.8.1, 4.8.2, 4.8.3, 4.8.4,
      4.8.5, 4.8.6
  academic institutions 4.8.2, 4.8.3
  continuing education 4.8
  in-house 4.8.6
  informal 4.8.6
  opportunities for staff 4.8.5
  self-help 4.8.1
  special courses 4.8.4
  Trustee Training Unit 4.8.6
Transfer of assets 2.6.1
  scheme 2.6.1.2
  statutory power 2.6.1.1
Treaties 5.2.1
Troubleshooting 4.9, 4.9.1, 4.9.2, 4.9.3,
    4.9.4, 4.9.5, 4.9.6, 4.9.6.1,
      4.9.6.2, 4.9.6.3, 4.9.7
  Charity Commission inquiry 4.9.6.2
  compensation 4.9.5
  emergencies 4.9.1
  insurance 4.9.2
  Lord Advocate's powers 4.9.6.3
  mediation 4.9.7
  negligence 4.9.3
  problems 4.9.6
  running out of money 4.9.6.1

Troubleshooting—*continued*
  tenants' defaults 4.9.4
Trust deed
  model A1
    application A1
Trust, charitable A1
Trustee meetings 4.2, 4.2.1, 4.2.2,
    4.2.3, 4.2.4, 4.2.5
Trustee Training Unit 4.8.6
Trustee(s) A1
  charity trustee A1, A2, A3
  committee
    charitable trust A1
    corporate charity A2
    unincorporated association A3
  disqualification
    effect A2
  first
    charitable trust A1
    corporate charity A2
  meetings and proceedings A1
  powers A1
    unincorporated association A3
Trustees 4.1, 4.2, 4.2.1, 4.2.2, 4.2.3,
    4.2.4, 4.2.5, 4.3, 4.3.1, 4.3.1.1,
    4.3.1.2, 4.3.2, 4.3.3, 4.3.4, 4.3.5,
      4.3.6, 4.4.10
  characteristics 4.1
  choosing 4.1
  meetings 4.2
    chairmanship 4.2.3
    frequency 4.2.5
    minutes 4.2.4
    preparation 4.2.1
    quorum 4.2.2
  professional advisers 4.3, 4.3.1,
    4.3.1.1, 4.3.1.2, 4.3.2, 4.3.3,
    4.3.4, 4.3.5, 4.3.6
  qualities 4.1
  relationship with director 4.4.10
Trustees' annual report B2

Unincorporated association
  constitution A3

Volunteers 4.4, 4.4.1, 4.4.2, 4.4.3, 4.4.4,
    4.4.5, 4.4.6, 4.4.7, 4.4.9
  encouragement or praise when
    deserved 4.4.4
  fairness 4.4.7
  freedom from annoyance 4.4.3
  freedom from insecurity 4.4.2
  health and safety legislation 4.4.9
  interviewing 4.4.1
  support for weaknesses 4.4.5
  training 4.4.6

Winding up 2.7, 2.7.1, 2.7.2, 2.7.3,
    2.7.4
  assets, charitable purposes A2
  charitable trust A1
  Charity Commission 2.7.4
  corporate charity A2

Winding up—*continued*
Court of Session 2.7.4
express power 2.7.1

Winding up—*continued*
scheme 2.7.3
statutory power 2.7.2